KU-636-276

Grateful acknowledgments are made to the following for permission to include prints and drawings of original prints, costumes and accessories: Welsh Folk Museum, St. Fagans; The National Museum of Wales; The National Library of Wales; Carmarthen, Tenby and Swansea Museums; The Glyn Vivian Art Gallery, Swansea; Brecon Museum; The Gower Society, and to Miss E. M. Evans and Mrs. Griff Morris for the use of authentic costumes.

Ken Etheridge

Welsh Costume

In the 18th & 19th century

Christopher Davies

This edition first published in 1977 by
Christopher Davies (Publishers) Ltd.
P.O. Box 403, Swansea, SA1 4YF

Fifth Impression 1997

ISBN 0 7154 0411 3

*Printed in Wales by
Dinefwr Press
Rawlings Road, Llandybïe
Carmarthenshire, SA18 3YD*

CONTENTS

A Gwent girl wearing a shawl (N.L.W.)

CHAPTER ONE

THE EIGHTEENTH CENTURY

WHAT we call national costume is based on the peasant costume of the eighteenth and nineteenth centuries. The dresses and accessories of the European countries, which are preserved on festival days and to impress the foreign visitors with their unique cut and design have little claim to originality apart from the colour and applied patterns, devised by the girls and women of the locality. Basically, they are all in line with the common dress of two hundred years ago; the advent of the industrial revolution made an end of home-made cloths and patterns, and very few of the idiosyncracies of the localities have survived today.

Welsh costume is no exception. It is fortunate in one respect that Wales has been isolated geographically from the rest of Britain; many of the individual traits of costume and materials were retained long after they had died out in the rest of Britain; but it must not be forgotten that the costume is really the common dress of the peasant, the farm servants and cottagers of bygone days. However picturesque they may appear to us today, many of these costumes were made for hard wear. Our survey will, therefore, deal with the costume worn in Wales in the last two centuries, and this is what we call "national costume", which is as individual and beautiful as any in Europe.

Rural Wales of the eighteenth century is described by many travellers. It was the day of the rambler and commentator who invariably wrote accounts of their travels. These descriptions are often very diverting:

"The women join more in the labours of the field than in England. A man holds the plow drawn by four horses, but oftener by 6 oxen and a girl drives them, sometimes she rides upon one of them. The men more generally drive the carts and wains, but the girls and women usually ride a horse and dragging a kind of sledge as used in Scotland."[1]

Another writer describes Swansea as a "clean, pretty-looking place, yet so little appearance of business and so few inhabitants that the grass was growing in some of the principal streets." At Llan-non he saw "cottages, many of them constructed of large stakes and wattled, then plastered over with a mixture of loam and cowdung . . . the upper part of the chimneys is of wattle work daubed over with clay, whitewashed a little without, but seldom ever within."[2]

Although the peasants lived very poorly, the gentry were well dressed and liked ostentation. They sometimes caused much eyebrow-raising by coming to church with servants in livery. Griffith Williams, Esq., "used to come to church with eight livery servants dressed in green and gold and made such a figure in a country church."[3]

These towns had civic pride, however, though they did not possess much in the way of amenities. The inhabitants joined together to celebrate any event which called for jollification in a big way: "The charter was brought to Carmarthen by the Hon. George Rice of Newton (Llandilo), M.P. for the county, and delivered to Albert Davids, Esq., the mayor named in the Charter." He would be dressed in his scarlet robes of office and

1. DIARY OF JOHN GRUBB, 1793.
2. Iolo Morganwg, 1796.
3. TOUR IN WALES, Journal of a Young Lady, 1788. Ms. N.L.W.

accompanied by his aldermen, similarly attired.[4] The account continues: "The inhabitants of the County Borough went in great pomp to meet their charter, in coaches and chariots, and near a thousand horses and men on foot innumerable, fifty-two white silk flags and three ravens drawn on each of them carrying a sprig of laurel in their beaks, signifying loyalty and good news; the three ravens being the arms of Dynevor Castle were carried by gentlemen's sons well mounted, and other flags by apprentices and others, almost innumerable with drums beating and divers other music. The charter being delivered to Albert Davids, Esq., at the town end of Abergwili bridge, he brought it to town with great joy in his coach, which was dressed with laurel, gilted with silver, etc." The Mayor then took the oath of office and other officers were sworn in. Jollifications followed: "An ox was roasted near the conduit in Lammas Street, and a sumptuous feast provided in the Long Store-house near the Quay, to which nearly 1,500 gentlemen and tradesmen sat down, the fragments were divided among the poor, and several hogsheads of ale and cider brought into the streets and given to the public. Bells were rung and cannons fired during the day; bonfires, fireworks and illuminations enlivened the night; the whole concluded with a ball, at which about a hundred couples danced."[5]

Town life was further enlivened by such spectacles as hangings. In 1739 Elinor Williams, a servant, was hanged for murdering her child and was afterwards gibbeted. In 1747 Captain Owens, a noted smuggler, was hanged. These were public events in those far-off days and the curious could see all the proceedings, even being permitted a view of the corpse, if they so desired.

Religious life was not particularly strong. A comment on churchgoing habits is made by the Rev. Nathaniel Jones,

---

4. "Here are a Mayor, two Sheriffs and Aldermen, all in scarlet gowns, with other ensigns of state." A NEW DESCRIPTION OF ALL THE COUNTIES IN ENGLAND AND WALES, 1741.
5. From CARMARTHEN AND ITS NEIGHBOURHOOD by William Spurrell.

writing of Merthyr Tydfil: "What devotion can they have that have their tobacco pipes in their mouths, when they go into the church, and are sneezing tobacco in the church when they come out after the sermon, they are smoking in the churchyard, going away, some to the ale-houses, others to tobacco houses."[6]

It could hardly be expected that the laity should lead good lives when their pastors were not always of exemplary character. The curate of Llanwinio is castigated as follows: "We hear by report of ye country he is defamed and scandalized by one Catherine Vychan, a vile and wicked woman and common strumpet, and by report mother of five or six bastard children and regards not to whom she fathers them." The question of the Curate's guilt or innocence in the matter of Catherine's children is not at all clear.

In other parishes there is fairly good behaviour. In Llanpumpsaint there seems to have been a resolution to improve the appearance of the church: "The floor of our church is uneven, but we design to cover it with earth very soon."[7] While at Llansadyrnin there is a parson "of exemplary life. He wears his own hair but of moderate decent length, and in apparel and behaviour grave and decent." This comment on the wearing of his own hair points to a sober habit among the Welsh clergy of the early eighteenth century; though they and their wives are severely lampooned by Twm o'r Nant later in the century for their extravagant dress and ways.

The question of selling things in the church-yard also seems to have been under review. Writes the clerk or curate of Cynwyl Elfed in 1720: "We know of none that sell wares on Sundays nor tipple in ale-houses in time of service."

Emotional extravagancies were to be expected in some places, when one considers the fiery nature of the Celt. "In

6. Rev. Nathaniel Jones, Ms.
7. TOUR IN WALES, Journal of a Young Lady, 1788. Ms. N.L.W.

these parts (near Llandovery) is a religious sect called Jumpers. They are most ignorant enthusiasts; after their extempore sermons, they jump and dance about the room in the most extravagant manner till they are quite exhausted. In these paroxysms some indecent familiarities between the sexes are said to take place, the usual conclusion of many religious transports." There were, however, genuine religious movements too, and Howell Harris toured the country in the course of his evangelical campaigns, unresting in his fight with the wickedness of the common people. "In this last journey, I have not taken off my clothes for seven nights," he writes to Mr. Baddington on October 20th, 1748, "travelling from one morning to the next evening without any rest above 100 miles, discoursing at midnight or very early on the mountains in order to avoid persecution."

There was a good deal of poverty in the country, and Howell Harris organised life at his Trefeca settlement to try to remedy this. Of the sixty members present in 1753, thirty-six of the women were engaged in picking wool, carding flax, spinning and knitting stockings. Flannel and dyed cloth made at their factory were sold at the markets in Brecon, Hay and Hereford. At the suggestion of Howel Harris the Breconshire Agricultural Society was formed in 1755. The sum of £400 was voted in 1758 to build eight looms in the county and the expenses of an expert flaxdresser from Scotland were paid to teach the men how to use the machines. Premiums were offered for making woollen cloths, dyeing and spinning, but the project did not pay its way and manufacturing cloth for home needs proved a failure.

Sheep-rearing was the main occupation of the country folk, and the produce of their sheep their main standby. Hard winters affected them cruelly. "This has been a very hard winter upon us mountain farmers; the losses among the sheep and lambs are very great indeed. I know not when to expect an end of it, for it snows and hails as fast as if it was the middle of

Fig. 1 (Left) Welsh gentleman of the 18th century, from Hogarth's THE ARREST. (Centre) Welsh farmers of Capel Curig from Pennant's "Journey to Snowdonia," 1791. (Right) A shepherd boy, from a water-colour by Rev. John Parker.

Fig. 2 (Left) Women knitting on tomen Y Bala, from Pennant's "Journey to Snowdonia." (Right) Pembroke women from an oil painting of the French invasion. (CM) They wear red shawls, dark brown betgwn and red petticoats.

December instead of April."[8] The people made up their own cloth and flannel, employing a local weaver and dyer. The occupations of a group of cottagers near Dolgellu in 1766 illustrate the ways of life in those days: 8 are weavers, 2 tanners, 2 shoemakers, 2 glovers, 2 masons, 2 tailors, 2 labourers; while there are: 1 gardener, 1 butcher, 1 carpenter, 1 clerk, 1 smith, 1 schoolmaster and 1 slater.

The homespun cloth produced by these cottagers was of a greyish, oatmeal or light of drab colour; flannel was natural white, light blue, cream or grey. They had the privilege of collecting wool from the hedges.

This gathering of wool fragments is described and the poor attire of the peasants may be noted: "For the Cattle feeding within the Covert and rushing through the Brake, every Briar took toll of their Coats and excis'd their Backs as fast as they filled their Bellies, on every Sprig there hung a Fragment of their Liveries, and the whole Hedge was cloath'd with tatter'd Fleeces as if wool had been vegetable and had grown there. These Spoils were look'd upon as excellent Booty to vagrant Youth, who went about stripping, plundering and, as it were,

---

8. Letter of Thomas Johnes of Hafod, April 15th, 1799.

16

sheep-shearing the Hedges, we met a crew of these Pickering Wool-gatherers; the very emblems of Beggary and but once remov'd from the vilest Rascality; one shoe apiece and half a Hat, a remnant of a Doublet and a moiety of a Sleeve, a Pair of Dispocket Breeches and a jagged Jump,[9] were the flower of their accoutrement, except two or three Locks of Wool, tuck'd like Scuts under their girdles, as a Badge of their Profession and some cramm'd Stockings bobbing at their Sides, as Trophies of their Pyracies."[10]

The material of the clothing is described as "freez"; no colour is mentioned, one may assume it was in the natural colour of the weave—light oatmeal or greyish white. "The materials of his Apparel are usually a well-shagg'd Freez, so that we cannot call it sleepy, being fleec'd with a Nap like any Sheep-Skin; it affords excellent Harbour to the Vermin of his Body, which, whether it be stock'd with Store of juicements for them, he commonly signifies by the Symbol of a Shrug."[11]

Further details are given of the form of the young Welshman's clothing: "His Fashion is generally a Pair of oblong Trouzers made of a Brace of Cloak-bags, suppos'd to be Twins; these, tack'd together, are a perfect Emblem of his crural attire. This garment had conjugal affinity to a thing call'd a Doublet of the same Lineage; copious Vestment, very Roomthy and Capacious, able to Comprehend both His Arms in the single Pudding-bag of one Sleeve; its uppermost confines were hemm'd with the scanty Dimensions of a contracted Collar, but its lower Exremity was bordered with the Paraphrace of amplified Lappets. The Summity of His Head is commonly pinnacled with the Battlement of a Button. Cuffs are an innovation. Things which their Ancestors were seldom guilty of, and indeed, Bands and clean Linnen are an upstart invention, being the modern Effect of Pride of their huge ones, whereas Primitive Britishment was never acquainted with the

9. A short coat or jacket. It was also worn by women instead of stays under the dress.
10. "TRAVELS AND MEMOIRS OF WALES," 1742.
11. Ibid.

17

Habilement of a Shirt. Their feet, it seems, are of an hot Complexion, for they often air their distockin'd Pettitoes; and if they had any hosen they were the offspring of their Drawers, to which they were fastened by Leathern Ligaments." This reference to bare feet again illustrates a habit of long usage among the Welsh; while the attempt to air an historical observation about the lack of shirts of the ancient Welsh betrays an ignorance of their ways; even in the Laws of Hywel there are frequent references to shirts, so we may discount this in the present writer's description, though his observations about his own times are no doubt true to life.

More exotic tints were also used. The dye-book of one Peter Price, dated 1767, contains notes of the following colours: "Scarlet, Cherry Colour, Ripe Apple Colour, Pink in the Grain, Pump y Dore (Dore-gilded?), Saxon Green and Blue Thread." His charges for dyeing were a shilling a yard for cloth and sixpence for flannel. Blue was a popular colour round Carmarthen; the town bellman used to wear a cloak of hand-woven blue cloth, made on a loom in Water Street. This cloak may still be seen at the Carmarthen Museum. Hand-looms used in the 18th century were capable of creating patterns in two colours—checks or stripes.

Weaving and spinning were carried out on the hearths. A description of a Welsh kitchen of 1773 tells of people listening to a harper, while a girl cards wool in the chimney-corner and rocks a cradle with her bare feet.[12] Linen as well as woollen cloth was a home-product, in fact the Welsh home was more or less self-contained, everything for the family's requirements in the way of food and clothing being produced locally or on the actual farm. Writes a Welsh lady of these times: "I will spin our wool and make stockings for Morgan (her son) and myself, and the weaver shall weave us a piece of Tilsy-wolsy (linsey-woolsey?) every year, and the taylor shall make Morgan a suit of clothes and me a gown, and we will sow our own flax and I

12. A letter in the ANNUAL REGISTER, 1773.

will spin that into shirts, shifts and sheets, and we will live so well and go so fine as we can. We will kill our own bacon, bake our bread and brew our own beer. Then we shall have everything of our own."[13]

The picture which accompanies this shows Mistress Shones riding on a goat with her son behind her. She is attired in a gown and a short jacket of darker material, and wears stout shoes and a large brimmed dark hat, with a bonnet under it. The gown of heavy cloth was worn all through the year. Defoe, writing in 1724, says that the women of Pembroke "even in the midst of summer wear a heavy cloth gown."

The clothing of the man was often called a "pair"—probably from the fact that it consisted of coat and trouser or breeches. Broadcloth could be bought in the towns by the richer farmers, but the clothing of the common people was home-spun material—woollen cloth for the suits and linen for the shirts, or flannel. The mention of shifts is interesting as it betokens a different night attire from the shirts worn in the daytime. This was probably so among the richer folk.

Clothing was often given as part of wages. This custom persisted down as far as the beginning of the 19th century and may have arisen from the local conditions—a farm-servant or man would find it very difficult to purchase clothing out of their meagre wages; woollen cloth was also difficult to obtain, as the lengths of cloth were made up from wool provided by the farmers and then returned to them by the weavers. An entry in a diary of 1708 reads: "Agreed with Anne Edward for her son for a whole year for a pair of clothes and a lamb."[14] Maid-servants received flannel for aprons; this clothing was in all probability made of homespun cloth, so did not cost the master anything out-of-pocket.

---

13. A broadsheet UNNAFRED SHONES. WIFE TO SHON AP MORGAN. The portrait is a caricature, but undoubtedly contains a true picture.

14. Diary of Rees ap Rees of Penrallt Kilbur, St. Dogmaels.

Fig. 3. A farmer and his wife of the 18th century from a broadsheet. (N.L.W.).

Details of articles of clothing worn by the common people may be gathered from vestry accounts and parish registers. One Elizabeth Richards wore "a jacket, shirt, petticoat and handkerchief and wooden shoes"; while Catherine Davies has "two new blankets, bedgown, petticoat and smock (shirt)" and Lettice Richard received a "flannel shift."[15] Wooden shoes are again mentioned for one Anne Clayton, who also received "two flannel shifts."[16]

The men wear "breeches" and one (William Thomas) has been allowed "2½ yards for a gwascod"; he also receives a pair of new wooden shoes.[17]

15. Tregaron Vestry Accounts, 1787-8.
16. Vestry Book of Llanfihangel y Creuddyn, 1791.
17. Ibid.

Fig. 4. Newcastle Emlyn women of the 18th century, from a water-colour by Ibbetson.

Fig. 5. Footwear of the 18th century Welsh girl. (Top left) A soleless stocking from a broadsheet caricature of Dame Wales. (N.L.W.) (Top right) A wooden patten. (C.M.). (Bottom) Shoes of black leather. (N.L.W.).

Paupers had to acknowledge their debt to the parish in no uncertain manner—by wearing a distinctive badge. We read of the purchase of "a yard of red flannel to put badges upon Ye Poor of ye Parish"[18] while a Lampeter Easter Vestry of 1783 ordered that paupers are to wear the customary letters L.P. (Lampeter Parish) upon their outward apparel. It is not clear how these letters were formed, but a will of 1728 gives us a clue. It bequeaths the income of certain lands up to £120 per annum in order to build almshouses for five decayed old men and five decayed old women, the balance to buy for them "an upper garment, which they shall be obliged to wear thenceforward publicly, with a brass badge on the left arm bearing the letters R.L."[19] So Richard Lloyd achieved some kind of immortality, if only in brass on the arms of paupers!

Even when in prison poor men and women were issued with clothing. A sad little tale may be gathered from the following items in the Glamorgan Records:[20]

	£	s	d
Paid for 12 weeks maintenance of a child left in jail, the Mother being transported at 1/6 per week	0	18	0
For a peticoate to the same		1	6
For 2 pairs of stockings			6
For mending shoes			6
For a coffin and shroud to a child that died in prison		7	0
To Parson, Clerk and Sexton and also for carrying to the grave		3	0

18. Llanyblodwel Parish Register, 1710.
19. Will of Roderick Lloyd of Merioneth, 1728.
20. Epiph, 1764.

21

There was no lessening of prison rigours because of sex. On January 1st, 1722, the Glamorgan Court ordered that "Gwenllian Jenkin, now a prisoner in his majesty's Gaol for the said County, convicted in this court for stealing a Silver Spoon be on Saturday . . the . . . day of this . . . between the hours of 10 and 12 of the clock in the morning of the same day, being first stripped from the waist upwards, well whippt."

To come back to particulars of costume: this varied a little in different parts of the country. The women of Gower wore dresses of a Flemish origin, seen, too, in the Tenby areas, consisting of a short jacket over a petticoat, a "whittle" being worn on top. This was a shawl-like piece of red cloth, fringed at one end. It was worn by women of the inland regions, too, as the following extract testifies: "Llanddarog women wear whittles, a very old fashion and bad, not for its age, but because the modern rural cloak is much more convenient and comfortable than the whittle; utility is the only thing that should fix fashions, nor should anything but a greater utility be permitted to change them; but let the Carmarthenshire lasses, retaining their perfect innocence and pleasing simplicity of manners—wear their whittles forever rather than run like some of the Glamorgan hare-brained wenches into the follies of fashion; ignorance of the English language guards many parts of Wales from a number of bad habits and from fashions . . ."[21] Llandarog—or Llanddarog as it is now called—is a village situated some seven miles east of Carmarthen. The retaining of the whittle may be due to poverty; the rural cloaks recommended by the writer and so much admired would need a good deal of material, which the average country girl could not afford.

The favourite colour in the coastal areas was red or scarlet, obtained from the cockle. The shawls or whittles were dyed this colour; flannel petticoats and jackets, too, contain a predominance of red, interwoven with black or cream pin-stripes.

21. Iolo Morganwg: JOURNAL OF AN EXCURSION INTO CARMARTHEN-SHIRE in June, 1796.

Welsh Girl in the Costume of Gower (N.L.W.)

Fig. 6 (Left) Gower girl of the 18th century, from an old water-colour. Artist unknown.
(Right) Mussel-gatherer of Llangwm with dress that shows Flemish influence. (T.M.)

Black check-patterns are seen in the shawls, too. Another
peculiarity of the Gower costume is the shape of the straw hat
and the rarity of the beaver, universally thought to be the
typical "Welsh hat". The straws of the Gower girls—black or
light yellow—have a flat top, which are useful for carrying the
baskets and pails. Pictures of girls with these on their heads are
frequent; the flat-crowned straws would be more convenient.
Another consideration is the prevalence of rough winds on the
coasts; a beaver hat would be very difficult to keep on; while
the close-fitting straw—frequently wrapped round with an
extra head-cloth—stays on the head.

A glimpse of the women of Aberystwyth is contained in the
following extract, from the pen of a young lady, writing at the
end of the 18th century, who says that the women "wear a petticoat and a jacket fitting close to the waist, of striped woollen,
and a man's hat. A blue cloak many of them had, but it is
reserved for dress, and in common they wear a long piece of
woollen cloth wrapped round the waist. I have a hundred times

24

seen a woman carrying a pitcher of water on her head, a child or loaf in this wrapper, and knitting as she walked along."[22] This striped material was in two shades of blue, seen in Aberystwyth costumes until the late nineteenth century.

Women of Pembroke again wear red shawls or wraps, which became famous during the "invasion" of 1798. Writes a commentator of this scare: "The country gathered from all parts of Pembrokeshire near four hundred women in red flannel and Squire Cambel (Lord Cawdor) went to ask them were they to fight and they said they were."[23] An oil-painting, said to have been painted about the time of the surrender of the French is to be seen at the Carmarthen Museum and contains little portraits of some of these Welsh Amazons holding the French at pitchfork point. The women wear red or dark brown shawls and skirts and blouses. One or two wear jackets, which have elbow-length sleeves. The heads appear to be wrapped in shawls or kerchiefs.

Another reference describe them as "poor women with red flannel over their shoulders, which the French at a distance took for soldiers, as they appeared all red."[24] Here it might be added that there were large military and naval forces in the area, too, and we must confess that the romantic story of the Welsh ladies forcing the French soldiers to surrender, is not entirely the truth.

The jacket or jerkin was worn in all parts of Wales as an upper garment. It originated perhaps in the overgown or dress of the seventeenth century. We see it depicted in drawings by Cox and Rowlandson as about threequarter length, reaching to or near the knee. Turner, Parker and John Warwick Smith also show girls wearing it. Almost like a blouse or jumper, gathered or cut to fit tightly to the waist, it is usually open up the front, fastening with buttons or invisible fasteners; some-

---

22. Miss Hutton, quoted by George Eyre Evans in his book, CARDIGANSHIRE AND ITS ANTIQUITIES.
23. From a letter of John and Mary Mathias of Narberth to their sister, February 27th, 1797.
24. Letter from John Mends, Haverfordwest, to his son John, February 27th, 1797.

times the part below the waist is a mere six-inch frill; at other times it is much longer, developing into a skirt. Perhaps the fashion changed with the wealth of the owner. A farmer's wife has a jacket reaching below her knees; a servant-girl wears one which is a mere six-inch frill below her apron-band. Sleeves and collars varied, too. Sleeves are mostly three-quarter length, some finish at the elbow with a deep cuff, fitting closely to the arm. The neck opening is V-shaped or round, cut so low sometimes as to reveal the undergarment or shift. A neckerchief or fichu could be worn to fill in the neck-line. The colours of Carmarthenshire were brick-red or crimson and black; those of Cardigan dark blue and red, or two shades of blue; Pembroke had clarets and dark browns, mixed with black; North Wales dark browns, yellows and violets, as well as innumerable greys and drabs are to be seen. Checks and squares of all shades of red and crimson are seen in Glamorgan, as well as the greys.

Fig. 7. Uniform of the Castlemartin Yeomen Cavalry, who met the French Invasion. Uniforms were blue with white facings, white gloves, brass buttons. Officers wore red coats with gold facings. Shakoes were black with plumes of white feathers or red and white horsehair. Details of the white braid and chain fastening are shown. (T.M.).

26

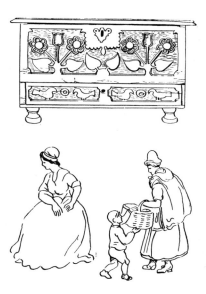

Fig. 8. (Top) A dower chest made in Gower in 1770. The design shows Flemish influence. (From "Gower Gleanings") (Bottom) Newcastle-Emlyn women, from a sketch by Rowlandson.

The skirt or petticoat worn underneath was ankle-length, shorter for young girls. It was cut fairly full, fitting closely to the waist. If a striped material was used, the stripes run vertically. The bottom hem might be enriched or strengthened with a braid, or with an extra thickness of the striped material sewn on with the stripes running horizontally. An additional frill would often be made by turning over the material and tucking it in—perhaps this was an economical way of adjusting the skirt to the changing height of the wearer; extra length could then be obtained by removing the tucks.

The shawl would add warmth to the shoulders; or a piece of flannel could be worn. Some pictures show this flannel wrapped round the waist first like a binder, then draped over the shoulders. (See fig. 4).

The head would be covered with a bonnet of white linen; sometimes with a straw hat or beaver on top. A writer of 1796 remarks of the Welsh women that they "wear a man's hat over a coiff or mop cap, or sometimes a coloured handkerchief—remarkable to see so many round hats on, for when they sit the backs of the seats are so high you cannot distinguish to which sex they belong."[25]

The bonnet of the Welsh girl was of a peculiar richness of design; the goffers or frills were very deep indeed. In a large household it was the work of one of the maids to keep these bonnets clean and tidily "goffered." To goffer meant the process of washing and starching the material then, while damp, poking the frills into shape with a "poking stick" of iron, or placing it inside a kind of machine called a "gofferer." This was a little wooden contraption consisting of two uprights about 6 to 9 inches apart with two pairs of grooves to contain the quills — cylindrical pieces of wood; these were arranged in two upright rows. To goffer the material, it was placed first over one quill, then round another, passing to and fro between the back row and front row quills until they were all used up, or the material had been placed in its entire length; then the top pair of quills were put in position and clamped into place with wooden wedges, and the whole thing put in front of the fire to dry. When the material was removed, it would remain in these flutings for some time. Damp and wear would affect the tidiness; then the frills would again be submitted to this process.

25. Sykes, 1796.

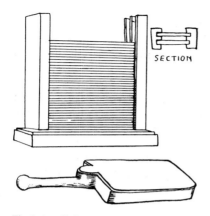

SECTION

Fig. 9. A goffering machine, used at Pen-parciau, Cardigan, in 1830. The quills are ⅜″. The damped starched material to be goffered was passed over and under the rows of quills in turn, starting at the bottom. The material was then allowed to dry before the fire in this position. (C.M.). (Below) A washing beetle or hand mangle, to beat or press clothes. It was used on a wooden roller or a flat stone by the riverside. (C.M.)

Fig. 10. A knitting-stick of white ivory. (N.M.W.).

These goffering machines vary in size. Some have quills about ⅜″ in diameter; others are ½″ or ⅝″. The poking irons, too, vary in thickness from about ¾″ to 1″ or 1¼″. These different sizes indicate the variations in the size of the frills. Pictures show this.

Stockings were hand-knitted; white, grey and black are seen. Wool of the black sheep was often used for stockings, and knitting-sticks were carved by lovers for the young ladies of their fancy. The stocking without a sole was often worn by

29

farmgirls, with a loop of wool round the big toe to keep it in place.

Wooden shoes have already been referred to. The practice among the poorer classes seems to have been to go about bare-footed. "The women are generally without shoes and stockings," wrote Sir Christopher Sykes; and the bare feet of the Welsh girls have aroused comment throughout the ages. Many drawings and paintings show them bare-footed; on the other hand Rowlandson's drawing of a kitchen-scene in New-castle Emlyn shows the men and women wearing boots. They are not very elegant, let it be admitted, still they are boots and low-heeled shoes. His girl washing clothes by the river Teifi has no shoes or stockings.

An amusing and interesting light on the making and mending of shoes is thrown by the following taken from the Old Gulston Account Book, Derwydd:

1708	s	d
Nov. 5th—Clogging up Miss		10
Dec. 4th—Mended up Miss		2
1709		
Jan. 9th—Toecapped Master		3
March 1st—Turned up, clogged up and mended Maid	1	6
Aug. 5th—Lined, turned up and put a piece in Madam	4	6
Sept. 6th—Soleing and covering up the Maid		6
Dec. 10th—Tapping Madam		6
Dec. 11th—Putting a piece in Madam		6
Dec. 12th—Stretching and easing little Master		7
Dec. 14th—Welting and stretching the Maid		10
Dec. 18th—Mending and patching the Cook		6

It is significant that the Mistress has shoes or boots with leather soles, while the maid has clogs as well. The "little Master's" shoes are of leather, too.

Pattens as well as shoes were worn around the house. Those of the eighteenth century are made of one piece of wood for the sole with uppers or straps of leather. An iron ring is attached to the sole by means of two bars, about 3 inches long, which raise the foot of the wearer off the ground; pattens are effective for

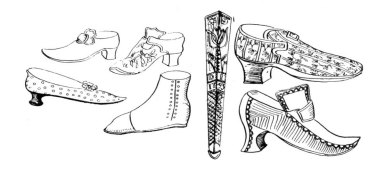

Fig. 11. Ladies' shoes of the 18th century (top left) from Meirioneth. The boot (bottom, left) is of dark blue satin, from Cardigan. Lacing is on the inside. (W.F.M.) The carved stay-busk is from Carmarthen, centre. (C.M.) The shoe (top right) is of lavender cloth with grey and red embroidery, heel dark red, from Meirioneth. The shoe, bottom right, is of cream satin with dark brown braid and heel, from Caernarvon. (W.F.M.)

keeping the feet dry and free from mud and dirt—a comment on conditions round the houses. Pattens were worn with the ordinary shoes by well-to-do people as well as maidservants. An account of 1744 gives details of pattens being paid for: "Paid for pattens and more are paid for my little Boy"—2s. [26] So it appears that the little boy of this family in the Vale of Aeron wore pattens, too.

The dress of the menfolk followed the cut and style of English fashions, homespun cloth being used. The "four grey coats" mentioned in a will of 1722, for bestowal among decayed persons, are probably the common wear of poor people[27]. Round Carmarthen blue cloth or flannel was the common wear; in the north, drab-coloured and dark grey seem more prevalent.

An inventory made in 1735 of the wardrobe of a Carmarthen

26. Household Accounts of Dorothy, Viscountess Lisbourne (Dorothy Glyn) while staying with her brother, David Lloyd, at Brynog, in the Vale of Aeron.
27. Will of Rev. Richard Drewes, Vicar of Meiford, 1722.

youth, deceased, gives an indication of the male attire of those days:

	s	d
5 shirts	5	0
2 suits clothes	8	0
1 hat	1	0
6 stocks	1	6
1 pr shoes	1	0
3 pr stockings	1	0

The "one pair shoes" is an interesting indication of the fashions of the time among Welsh people—probably a best pair worn only on special occasions. The five shirts are remarkable, to say the least, combined with the six stocks (cravats) indicate a fastidiousness in linen wear, which we find exemplified again in the famous Beau Nash, born at Swansea and educated at Carmarthen Grammar School.

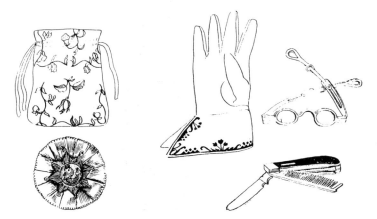

Fig. 12 (top). A white satin handkerchief satchel, embroidered dark green, blue, rose and pale green. (W.F.M.). (Bottom) Badge worn by the Society of Sea-Sergeants, a Jacobite faction. The badge is of silver, ribbon pale blue satin. (T.M.).

Fig. 13 (left). A doeskin glove of the early 18th century. (W.F.M.). (Right) Brass spectacles of the Rev. Peter Williams, and knife and comb of Rev. William Morus. (N.M.W.).

Welsh girl in the costume of Gower. (N.L.W.).

The influence of Beau Nash at the beginning of the century was a salutary one among the ladies and gentlemen of society in fashionable Bath; he decreed that women should not wear aprons and that men should not carry swords at social functions. While acting as Master of Ceremonies, he himself wore a tall white hat. Perhaps the decree about aprons recalled his own fastidious horror to see his native cousins in their flannel aprons, used for all purposes and on all occasions.

The upper classes in Wales copied the English fashions and bought stuff at town shops to make their dresses and appurtenances. The accounts of Viscountess Lisbourne, referred to above, contain details of stuffs bought, including cambric, silks, laces, ribbon, dimity and muslin. The item most often mentioned is cambric; nine yards are bought altogether in the course of the year for the use of two ladies; muslin is purchased, too, "a yard and a half for Mr. Lloyd for two cravats" indicates that it was used for articles of male attire as well as by the ladies.

Other items of interest are:

	s	d
"Paid for cloth to make Mr. Lloyd and Miss Lloyd shifts	12	0
"2 large handkerchiefs, one for Miss Lloyd one for myslef	5	6
"6 yards of Dimity for myself	6	0
"Paid for a pair of thread stockings for Mr. Lloyd	2	6
"Paid for as much calico as made me a gown	17	0

The price of calico in another item is given as 5s 6d. for 4½ yards of material for her gown, which obviously followed the fashions of that time in fullness and length. The four yards of ribbon, fine thread, and quilting may refer to the same gown.

Another interesting item states: "Paid for tea and mending my stays, 6s. 0d" which makes one wonder whether the mending of the stays was undertaken by the same person who sold the tea—probably the local haberdashery stores.

Other payments are made for "making 4 gowns" and also to

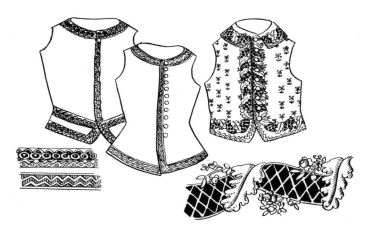

Fig. 14. Waistcoats worn by Welshmen of the 18th century, from Tredegar Park. (Left) Grey satin with silver, black and grey border. (Centre) Grey satin with silver braid. (Right) Cream satin with olive, pink and bronze embroidery, gilt buttons. (W.F.M.)

"Richard the tailor," which indicate that local seamstresses and tailors were employed.

Footwear is often mentioned; payments being made for "stockings" and also "thread stockings" for Mr. Lloyd—probably cotton stockings.

Portraits of the Welsh gentry of these times show them attired in the latest London fashions. The portrait of Sir Watkin Williams-Wynn, painted by Batori in 1768, depicts him as wearing a pink satin coat with gold braid facings down the centre and on the edges of the pockets, the sleeves being cut to the elbow. His cambric shirt has white lace cuffs and white lace at the neck. On top he wears an olive-green satin cloak, lined with a dark fur and fastening with a green silk cord. Black velvet breeches, white stockings and black shoes with silver buckles complete the gentleman's outfit, which combines colour and elegance. Some embroidered waistcoats are illustrated in figure 14.

These gentlemen bought their clothing from London firms, as can be seen from the following letter from Saunders and Skidmore, York Buildings, London to John George Phillipps, Esq., M.P., of Cwmgwili, near Carmarthen:[28]

2 November, 1789.

Sir,

The remainder of your order I received from Mrs. Saunders, viz., a blue-gray uniform frock with two white kerrseymere waistcoats, with two pairs of ditto breeches; also two pairs of worsted Valencia breeches, which shall be sent by this evening's mail coach."

Wigs were worn in common with the gentry of England. When the tomb of Sir Richard Steele was re-opened during repairs to St. Peter's Church, Carmarthen at the end of the last century, a silken ribbon with which he used to tie up his wig was found. He was buried in 1729. "The skull was very well preserved and bore a periwig with a bow of black ribbon tied at one end."[29]

Personal ornaments, such as rings, are often mentioned in wills and bequests. Baron Richards of Dolgellau had a gold collar of 'S's' which he wore over his robes. Sir Tomas Powell, Broadway, Laugharne, bequeathed to his "daughter Elizabeth, the diamond ring I usually wear" and "to my son Herbert, a signet ring of gold which has my coat of arms quartered and engraved upon it . . . and also another gold ring with a green stone, under which is enclosed a lock of my late most honoured father's hair." The position of the wife is suggested by the following item from the same will: "To my wife Judith, all her jewels she usually wears, only I desire the knot of diamonds may be continued as an heirloom in the family as it long hath been."

---

28. TRANSACTIONS OF THE CARMARTHENSHIRE ANTIQUARIAN SOCIETY, Vol. III, 1907.
29. Cwmgwili MSS.

That the lower orders tried to copy the fashions of the wealthy is shown clearly in the satires of Twm o'r Nant (Thomas Edwards), the writer of the interludes. He criticises the servant girls for their eagerness to purchase "many coloured gowns and stays, whatever the shirt may be like, a shaggy hat, frilled bonnet, however ugly they may be." They also indulge in "black satin cloak and wire caps, balloon bonnets and ribboned hats, large handkerchiefs and double frills", while they must have a "caroline hat", fine shirts and silk mufflers and velvet collars on their coats in order to gain respect among their lovers. He concludes his diatribe with a satiric couplet:

> "The pride of foolish Welsh people
> Imitates that of the English."

These may have been the clothes worn by the girls on Sundays. An eighteenth century saying from Llanbryn-mair describes the best clothes as "dillad cig rhost"—"clothes for roast meat"—an allusion to the fact that roast meat was on the bill of fare on Sundays, when the best clothes would be worn.

Welsh girls were very good embroiderers; aprons, handkerchiefs, cases, wallets and detachable pockets were all beautifully worked in coloured silks; the aprons were of ivory satin with designs in shades of bronze, purple and green. The wallet with designs of drums and banners may be for a soldier.

Cardiff girls are depicted in a painting by Thomas Rowlandson. They wear beaver hats with crowns of about seven inches, square in shape, and also poke bonnets; some wear brown skirts or kirtles over a white petticoat; others wear tight-waisted short-sleeved coats. One or two wear red cloaks with hoods, about knee length. Men in the painting wear the same kind of square beaver hats, with knee-breeches and coats of brown. (N.M.W.).

Fig. 15. (Left) An apron of ivory satin, made at Laugharne in 1720, with purple, grey, lavender and bronze silks. (Right) A white linen wallet embroidered in crimson, dark green, blue and yellow silk. (W.F.M.).

A painting by Paul Sandby shows the Cardiff girls again wearing brown and white striped skirts, and dark blue over-dresses tucked up. A little girl wears a tight-waisted blue blouse. White aprons are seen, long-sleeved blue coats and red cloaks similar to those in the Rowlandson drawings. One woman wears a pair of boots reaching almost to the knees; the other wears shoes. Kerchiefs are worn under the hats.. A little boy wears blue stockings, fawn breeches, dark brown or black coat and white shirt.

Llangollen costume of a milkmaid is shown in a painting by Ibbetson. She wears a white-frilled bonnet, white blouse, white neck-cloth with a blue kirtle (tucked up) and a red underskirt. White stockings show underneath, and black shoes.

Another girl at Ewenny Priory (in a painting by Turner), wears a brown-and-white striped skirt, blue-and-white striped petticoat, white bonnet and white blouse or shirt.

Bala girls wear red cloaks according to Jack Glan-y-gors, who wrote to a friend, May 16th, 1798, that while at Bala fair he "had the honour of making love to two ladies with red cloaks."

Red is a fairly prevalent colour in underskirts or petticoats. A girl in the region of Trapp (Carmarthenshire), is shown in a painting by David Cox, wearing a red underskirt and a blue blouse with elbow-length sleeves. She is bare-footed. A shepherd in the background wears brown-grey coat and breeches, which look like homespun material (G.V.). Another painting by David Cox shows haymakers wearing brown skirts, dark blue stockings and blue-grey blouses with tight waists. One girl wears a bonnet, one a hat and a white apron. A neckerchief of white material is also worn.

Country men wore linen smocks. A painting by the Rev. John Parker shows a shepherd near Bala wearing a smock, red muffler and blue stockings. Another smock in the National Museum, Cardiff, originally from Cardigan, is of natural crash with long sleeves and smocking on chest and cuffs; another has an additional shoulder-piece like the cape on a great-coat; the cuffs are fastened with two bone buttons and the neck opening with four buttons; a third type fastens all down the front with buttons.

Welsh Costume showing a range of tall hats (N.L.W.)

Chapter Two

THE TALL HAT

The origin of the tall hat (or beaver hat) in Wales has long been a subject of controversy among historians. Lord Raglan in *The London Mystery Magazine* traced its origin to the hats worn in the seventeenth century—a fashion retained by the gentry of Wales after it has passed away in England; but this kind of hat seems to me to be quite different from the one we now know as the Welsh hat.

There are many paintings and drawings of Welsh girls wearing the tall beaver in the nineteenth century, but the earliest of these date from the beginning of the century when the hat appeared to become very popular. Its price, however (about five guineas at that time), made it prohibitive except to the fairly wealthy farmers and their wives and daughters, and it was a luxury item rather than a necessary part of native costume. Many girls, in fact the majority, appeared to favour the bonnet, the straw and the low-crowned felt hats; while the shawl over the head was a fairly common form of head-covering in country areas. The large shawl (which we know now as the nursing shawl) lent itself to this fashion.

Perhaps a ballad of the late seventies may give us a clue. This ballad was printed in a collection in 1778[1] and must have had currency in Wales for some years earlier; so we may conclude

---

1. N.L.W.

that the tall hat had become fashionable by this time. The writer of the ballad deals with dress in general and criticises in particular the extravagant head-dresses; ladies are ridiculed for wearing the "maccaroni," which here signifies the tall wig worn by dandies of fashion; and for carrying large pots on their heads (the hats). I quote parts of the ballad in a free translation:

> Every lady, prinked and proud
> Her head with maccaroni showed
> In wondrous plaits of woven hair.
> O, hard it is to praise the fair!
> The sprightly miss, all sense defied,
> Will pay a salty price for pride.

> Now many a lady, gay and fair,
> Throws to the roof her lofty hair,
> And smiles so slyly now, alack,
> To see the ceiling throw it back.

> If ladies heads get any bigger,
> The doors will not contain the figure.
> There'll be no room for them to bide:
> They'll have to gossip all outside.

The writer then goes on to quote similar enormities in early Britain and mentions a tribe called the "Coriniaid" who were destroyed because "they were troubled with large heads and nursed sickness in the roots of their hair." (This may refer to the long hair worn by the early Celts—as late as Tudor times the Irish peasants were described as wearing their hair very long and thick, the matted mass acting as a protection against blows and weather). England, says the writer, had spared itself this humiliation, but there had come to Wales:

44

An ugly fashion, widely spread,
Of clapping pitchers on the head.
Fie on the wayward girls of France,
Who started this extravagance!

This line makes it clear that the fashion originated in France (according to the ballad-singer), though one has to accept this judgement with caution; it must be pointed out, however, that there was current in France of the late eighteenth century a fashion of wearing high hats. The ladies of the Court of Louis XVI wore such high hats when out riding to cover their elaborate periwigs. Like their cousins across the channel, it was the wealthier ladies who copied the fashion:

The blustering farmers ride to town,
Beribboned queue and cap on crown.

The "queue" meant here a wig with a tail, which was decorated with ribbons.

The country girls with simpering sigh
With English cousins now must vie;
These lofty crowns, these wigs and bows
Will be just right to scare the crows.
These gewgaws put them in a passion
To make them all the slaves of fashion;
They work so hard from early dawn
To buy a lace or finest lawn
And shudder as with fever's rack
To see it coarse—and send it back.
See them on Sunday at the glass;
Their heads are all a ribboned mass.
The ugliest wenches in the world
Must have fine raiment, crimped and curled.

The ballad goes on to decry the tall hats, describing them as:

> Palace for cats, a mouse's home;
> Secrets are in this horsehair dome!
> O, shame it is such sins to see
> On hot heads, carried thus with glee,
> A pound in weight. What can be done,
> But take a pot-shot with a gun?
> Out of Annoon this fashion came:
> Cast it from favour into flame
> Or wrest it from its boat of wool
> And into little pieces pull
> This basket, only fit for dung,
> Or on a ballad-singer hung
> To house his wares. This sack from hell
> We should not buy, and scorn to sell
> Such rags of scarecrows as they dance!
> O, send it back again to France!

This suggests that the tall hat went with the wig and ribboned caps, popular at the end of the eighteenth century. It is significant, however, that the derision voiced in this ballad did not affect the popularity of the tall hat; in a few decades it was widely worn; pictures of the larger towns, such as Bangor, Swansea and Cardiff, show many women wearing it. A print of Llanberis peasants and farmers shows a farmer's wife wearing such a beaver hat and the maidservant looking on with envy.

Many hats may still be seen. One at Carmarthen Museum bears the name "Andre" inside the rim, a Paris hatmaker. They were also made locally; cheap imitations in felt and straw were manufactured in cottages and carried to the local markets. Many old ladies in the locality carried on such a trade. The more expensive Paris moderls were beautifully lined with white or grey quilted silk, the cheaper ones had plain calico or lawn. The original hat was oval in shape and fitted the head perfectly. It was worn with the line of the brim level with the eyebrows, not at the back of the head.

Fig. 16. A Welsh wedding of the 18th century, from a print in "The Briton Described," or a "Journey Through Wales."

The men wear long-sleeved waistcoats, breeches and stockings, the girls ankle-length dresses with tight bodices, full skirts.

Fig. 16a. (Left) Linen smocks with stitching and smocking in white thread. (Top) New Cross, Aberystwyth; (centre) Llanfilo, Brecon; (bottom) Dolgellau. (W.F.M.)

Fig. 16b. Baby's bonnets 1800-1850. (Top) Pale blue lace; (left) Cream crocheted wool; (right) White lawn and lace. (B.M.)

CHAPTER THREE

THE NINETEENTH CENTURY

"Rarely have I seen so truly sweet a spot on a high road. The cottages, all whitened in front and scattered carelessly about, stud the sides of the hills on each side, a group of cottagers, it being Sunday, here and there on benches under the shade, while the Welch girls in men's black hats, with are universally worn among the common people, saluted us as they cantered by on their ponies."[1] So wrote a traveller in Wales in the early nineteenth century.

Another traveller wrote of Carmarthenshire: "The walk from Cross Inn (now called Ammanford) to Llandebie is very beautiful, at the latter place I put up at the Red Lion and experienced the greatest comfort and cleanliness; with the most moderate charges I ever met with in my life, I had a pint of good new milk, a bottle of excellent Welsh ale, roasted potatoes, bread, cheese, butter and an admirable bed for 1/6."[2]

Wales had by this time lost a good deal of its individuality owing to the improved communications. There were two mail coaches from Carmarthen to London; leaving every night at 9 o'clock as early as 1822; one of these went via Swansea and one via Gloucester. A coach also left for Milford and Ireland every

1. James White, friend of Charles Lamb, PICTURESQUE EXCURSION INTO SOUTH WALES, 1805.
2. Diary of Captain Jenkin Jones (unpublished) Ms in National Library of Wales, dated 1819.

morning at four o'clock and there was a horse post to Cardigan on four days a week, returning the same evening (Sunday, Tuesday, Wednesday and Friday), so it was possible for gentlemen and their families to keep in touch with the fashions of the metropolis. There were, however, many old customs still in existence, and home-made clothes from the wool of the native sheep was the wear of the common people of the rural areas.

Each area specialised in its own kind of cloth; Gwallter Mechain tells us that blue cloth was woven in Anglesey and sold at Chester fair; while the people of Caernarvon produced two kinds of cloth—a blue cloth to sell in Merioneth, and a grey (called "brethyn Sir Fôn"—the cloth of Anglesey) to sell at the Anglesey fairs. The finest flannel was made in the district between Dolobran and Llanidloes, which was called the Welsh flannel country. A kind of slate-blue flannel was produced in the Carmarthen district, while the coastal regions of Gower, Llanelli and southern Glamorgan specialised in the production of a brilliant scarlet cloth; in Pembroke it was dark red, almost claret; in Gower it was more scarlet; in Carmarthen and Llanelli (Penclawdd) it was more of a crimson colour; all were sometimes striped with narrow lines of black, cream, white or dark brown. In Montgomery cloths of blue, drab and brown—all with stripes of darker self-colour—were produced.[3]

Perhaps this choice of colour had a good deal to do with local products; the red, obtained in earliest times from the cockle, was a colour predominating near the coast; while blacks and browns from rock lichens were the colours worn by shepherds and their families in the mountain regions. The relation between dye and the vegetation of the locality was probably much more distinct in the olden days of restricted communications. With the advent of industrial amenities the local idiosyncrasies tended to vanish.

3. F. N. Potts GAZETTEER, 1810.

A few of the larger towns had established cloth-making factories. Caerphilly wove yard-wide cloths and broad-cloth; Bridgend produced serge, plush, plains and kerseys from the fine wool of the Glamorgan vales; while other items were manufactured at Denbigh (shoes and gloves), Monmouth (caps), and Mold (cotton goods); Holywell produced silks and cottons, while boots and shoes were produced at Narberth, Haverfordwest and Lampeter. Many of these towns still produce hand-made articles today.

An attempt was made to encourage home industries by offering premiums. The Agriculture And Industry Society was formed in 1800 and gave awards to cottagers and husbandmen and their families, who showed diligence and skill. Premiums were awarded to:

"David Evans, of the parish of Penboir, cottager, for having, with his wife and children, spun 299 lbs. of yarn and wool from the 1st day of January, 1800, to the end of the same year — £2. 2s. 0d.

"Margaret Daniel, of the parish of Llangeler, cottager, for having spun 123 lbs. of yarn and wool for the same period—£1. 10s. 0d.

"Anne Rees, of the parish of Penboir, cottager, for having in the same time spun 120 lbs. of wool and yarn, and knitted 19 pairs of stockings—£1. 5s. 0d.

"To Hannah Thomas, of the parish of Llangeler, Carmarthen, for having during the same time spun 57 lbs. of wool and yarn and knitted 51 pairs of stockings—£0 15s. 0d."[4]

The mention of stockings shows that this was still a much-practised rural occupation.

---

4. Transactions of the Carmarthenshire Antiquarian Society, Vol. XIX.

Another body that tried to encourage the woollen industry was the National Eisteddfod, which offered in 1845 prizes at the Abergavenny function for:

Rodney woollen

Welsh woollen whittle

Welsh woollen for dress

Blue cloth for a cloak

Best specimen of colours in Welsh yarn dyed in Gwent or Morgannwg or any other part of S. Wales.

Best woollen waistcoat piece

Best pair of women's knitted stockings.

Best lady's beaver hat.

Fig. 17. Girls of North Wales washing clothes. (N.L.W.)

To follow the process of wool manufacture from sheep to cloth-maker is a fascinating study, bringing into the picture local customs and traditions. In the Black Mountains—to take an example—old customs dating to the middle ages, and probably earlier, still remained. The yearlings were driven to the uplands at the beginning of April, and driven down again at the beginning of June, collected and washed in a river pool, then they were kept in a nearby field and sheared. Each farm would work on successive days, one family helping the other. Lambs were shorn at the end of August fifty years ago, but now it is done at the same time as the washing. Sheep were collected again at the end of August for dipping, again a communal task in which all would help.

A good deal of the work of preparing the wool was done by hand in the old days. First it was combed with teasels which were specially grown in cottage gardens for this purpose. One often sees the plant growing wild near the site of old mills and cottages. The teasel heads were put side by side in a little wooden frame; this custom continued until the advent of the machine, which came to the remoter districts quite late in the century, replacing the teasels with steel points. The wool was then passed on to the spinner, who worked for long hours turning the combed wool into threads, by her side a little candle on its iron bracket to light the dark chimney corner of the kitchen. As late as 1893 the Welsh cottage woman was constantly occupied in carding, knitting and spinning; while the children were kept busy, too; they had the privilege of collecting wool from the hedges and picking up the bits that were left after the shearing.[1] Every house had its spinning-wheel, and hand-looms were housed in lean-to buildings attached to farms.

The wool then passed to the weaver, who was a craftsman venerated by all for his skill, which took a lifetime to learn. He

1. GLIMPSES OF WELSH LIFE AND CHARACTER, Marie Trevelyan, 1893.

was practised not only in the weaving, but also in dyeing and fulling the cloth. The dyeing varied in different regions (as indicated above); checks and stripes were also peculiar to certain localities and not to others. Checks were popular in the eastern parts of the country and in the northern parts of Cardigan, while plaid patterns were prevalent in Gwent. Altogether South Wales patterns and colourings were considerably gayer; scarlet, crimson, blues and orange and bright browns were seen; while in the North drabs, greys and black, with greens, Prussian blues and violets (in the Bangor area) were more prevalent. Herbs, plants and wild fruit, such as blackberry and bilberry were used; onion skins gave a rich brown; indigo gave a variety of blues and greens; chemical dyes superceded the vegetable, but it is doubtful whether any more beautiful or lasting colours were achieved.

The indigo dye was imported. A list of the cargo of a ship wrecked off the coast of North Wales includes indigo.[2] The dye appears to have been ground by hand before use by the dyers; a canon ball weighing 16¾ lbs. was purchased by the Carmarthen Museum in 1892, which had been used for grinding indigo by the dyer at Llandyfan Forge (near Trapp). He said he had purchased the cannon ball from a party who had found it near Carreg-cennen Castle and he had used it for the past twenty years. This man, William Lewis, had attained some eminence as a weaver and dyer, for he had in 1851 made Welsh costumes for two figures (male and female) to send to the Great Exhibition. The figures had been modelled from his son and daughter.[3]

The wool of black sheep was used in North Wales, the sheep being specially reared for this purpose, giving wool of a peculiar smoky-black, which is very pleasant combined with other colours. It was used mostly for stockings, perhaps be-

2. Letter of Richard Thomas, Anglesey.
3. Diary of Thomas Jenkins, Llandeilo Fawr.

cause the wool, being its natural colour had no dye to lose by frequent washing.[4]

Fulling of the cloth was carried out in the earliest times by means of a large trough, which was filled with water or urine; the latter was collected from the houses, which kept the "slops" for this purpose. Fullers earth was used, too, and soap. The cloth was processed by the men walking over it, bare-footed, the process being carried out three times. The cloth was then put out to dry on hooks on a kind of wooden rail or fence near the factory. These drying rails may still be seen near old factories, usually placed in a sunny spot on an open field.

After fulling and drying, the cloth was put in a press, the folds having paper in between. It was then passed on to the tailor to make a "pair of clothes"[5] (*par o ddillad*). This was the term used by the country people for a man's suit and anticipates the modern "two-piece," the wear of the average worker was this suit consisting of coat and trousers or breeches.[6]

A travelling tailor undertook the making of the clothes. He was the repository of all the news, gossip and wonderful and salacious happenings of the locality and would work his way from farm to farm, "dates" being made by word of mouth or by message; he would also work in the houses of the village where he lived. The tailor of bygone Wales had his own methods, scorning the inch-tape and paper pattern. "Line and patterns they were not acquainted with . . . the tailor's tape-measure would be an old newspaper cut into strips about half an inch wide, stitched together to make a suitable length, he would cut special marks on the edge of the line to denote the different length and measurement. The square and the pattern he was not acquainted with at all; sometimes the tailor would measure the joint of the arm with his hand; he would grip a man's shoulder with his left hand, place the ends of his fingers and

4. RADNORSHIRE, W. H. Howse.
5. Y CREFFTWR YNG NGHYMRU, Iorwerth Peate.
6. Apprentices received "one pair of clothes" at the time of indenture. Llanarthney Parish Vestry.

thumb in that position on the cloth, marking with chalk a circle round the fingers with his right hand. Sometimes he would put a bowl face downwards on the cloth or material, or a horseshoe perhaps, to mark the shape of the arm-socket."[7]

Fig. 18. Hairstyles of Welshmen of the mid-19th century, Rev. T. R. Walters and Rev. Latimer Maurice Jones, of St. David's and Carmarthen.

Fig. 18a. Cardigan man of 1850. (N.M.W.) wearing coat of black broadcloth, cream waistcoat, rib trousers and grey knitted stockings. Buttons are brass.

The cloth was usually homespun, made from the wool of sheep reared on the farm. It was truly *brethyn cartre*—home produced cloth. "A farmer might look at his finished suit and say 'See the cloth of this coat, it is the wool of the two grey-poll sheep. The wool of the *llwdn cwta* (short-haired sheep) is in the

---

7. Gwilym Hiraethog.

waistcoat. The wool of the upper coat is a bit coarser—the wool of the short-horn'.["8]

Fig. 19. (Left) Bonnet of white lawn from Portmadoc, by kind permission of Mrs. Griff Morus. (Centre) Stocking of pale blue silk, worn by a lady of Plas Llanfair. (Top right) Bonnet of cream figured satin with wired brim and lace edge. (Bottom right) A carved knitting-stick from Caerphilly. (W.F.M.).

In the same way, dressmakers catered for the ladies, and girls learned their trade by being apprenticed to them. An advertisement in a Radnor paper of 1822 reads:

"Respectable young person wanted as apprentice to dressmaker—the young person's morals would be strictly attended to."

It is a matter of speculation how near these products were to the current London styles; illustrations of country girls show a good deal of variation in cut and design, while the fashions in bonnets and straws and beavers alone would fill a very long chapter. The variations may be studied in the illustrations.

8. RADNORSHIRE, W. H. Howse.

Considered generally, the dresses consisted of two parts—the *betgwn* and the *pais* (bedgown, a loose upper garment, and the petticoat). These were by no means peculiar to Wales; they were worn by peasant classes in the North of England[9] and also on the continent.[10] Their individuality lies in the choice of materials and in the local colourings. The *betgwn* and *pais* were supplemented with aprons, fichus and shawls of great variety.[11]

The *betgwn* varied in shape; sometimes it was short, as worn by the Pembroke girl and other farm-servants, differing little from that of the 18th century.

Later in the century the *betgwn* lost its skirts altogether and developed into the short blouse—as in the Carmarthen example. At the beginning of the century the skirts were long and full, two wide pleats at the back giving extra fullness, like those of a riding habit, upon which the *betgwn* is probably based. This pattern is seen in the Pembrokeshire example, illustrated. A row of smaller pleats were sometimes put in instead. The front corners were then raised and pinned or buttoned to the small of the back. Two small, flannel-covered buttons were sometimes placed here for the purpose. The hems of skirts and petticoats were finished with braid of a matching or contrasting colour. Yokes were round or V-shaped. Sleeves leg-o'-mutton or cut close-fitting to the elbow; sometimes they were threequarter and fairly wide, as in the costume of the Lampeter and Glamorgan girls.

Additional sleeves were sometimes made to attach to the half-sleeve. The sleeves of the *betgwn* are short, but two

9. Sir Walter Scott.
10. Lady Charlotte Guest's Diaries.
11. Lady Llanover's essay of 1836 "to encourage the preservation of Welsh language and costume" did not describe the "betgwn" and "pais" as national dress but gave them praise for neatness and durability.

detachable sleeves of black alpaca are fitted on at the elbow. Bows of black ribbon at the top indicate that the sleeves could be tied on to those of the *betgwn*. This costume was worn by a farmgirl. After the rough work had been done, she would attach these more elegant sleeves to her dress, giving an extra touch of smartness. The long sleeves would otherwise get in the way during work. The sleeves, illustrated, are lined and have a double cuff at the bottom with a facing of black silk. They were also made of plain linen or knitted.[12]

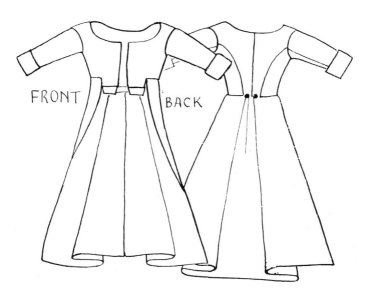

Fig. 20. Pattern of the *betgwn*, from an original Cardigan costume, by kind permission of Miss E. M. Evans. The lower hem is 71″ wide and is bound with black silk. There is a box-pleat at the back with two small buttons, covered with material. The outer corners in front can be fastened here, or tucked in underneath. The cuffs are covered with black silk. Material is of dark red flannel with a black stripe. The stripes run vertically on the skirt and bodice and across the sleeves. Bodice is lined with white calico.

12. Diary of Mr. Masleni, description of Carmarthen girl.

The illustration of the Caernarvon girl so dressed shows her wearing these detachable linen sleeves, which appear to be gathered on a tape at the elbow and tied into place. These are not attached to the sleeve of the dress at all.

The petticoat did not vary very much in style or cut. It was ankle-length, made fairly full. Two or three tucks were sometimes added at the bottom for extra heaviness, and the top was gathered into a plain black or grey band to fit the waist. If a striped material was used, the stripes usually went vertically, although examples of horizontal stripes have been seen. The bottom edge could be stiffened with a deep hem, braid or caddis, in a matching or contrasting colour. As this was usually on the inside it was not very much seen. It saved the edges from fraying and gave added protection. The more affluent women had more elaborate petticoats; the Bangor farmwife is seen wearing one of a pale lavender quilted silk—it looks like a fashion of the eighteenth century. For everyday wear the most popular colour was red; in all parts of the country the petticoat shows as scarlet or crimson. This preference for scarlet may have something to do with the durability of this colour or with the superstition that red was warmer to wear than other colours. Red flannel is an old remedy for a cold, for rheumatism or colic and also a protective in cases of fever. A red flannel petticoat put over the window of a sick room, was considered a certain cure for fevers. There were probably magical associations, too. Fairies in folk-lore are sometimes depicted as wearing red.

SHAWLS

On top of the dress was worn the shawl, which varied a good deal according to the locality. Sometimes the shawl was quite small "turnovers"—about twenty inches square, seen in Llanelli by Marie Trevelyan, and also at Cardiff and Tenby. These were folded diagonally to form a triangle and worn with one corner hanging down the back and the two others meeting or folded over the front. A pin or brooch held the shawl in

Fig. 21. Farmwife and servant of Caernarvon. The farmwife wears a quilted petticoat of lavender satin, a red underskirt and a *betgwn* of dark blue. Her shawl is yellow with red and green patterns, hat black with red ribbon, apron white, shoes black. The servant girl wears a blue *betgwn* with crimson stripes, green petticoat with red and black stripes. Her clogs are wooden-soled, coloured pink, with black uppers, sleeves pale yellow with black spots, shawl cream and black. (N.L.W.).

place. Old prints of Cardigan scenes also show the shawls worn in this way.

Other shawls were much larger, for example the Gower whittle, which was red or reddish brown in colour and worn in a variety of ways—over the shoulders to join in the centre, wrapped round the waist, enfolding the arms, etc. A large shawl was used, too, to wrap up or nurse a baby in the Welsh fashion. The shawl was folded in half across its width—or sometimes diagonally—then one end wrapped round the child, while a helper would hold out the other. The mother would then take the child in her left arm and the helper would wrap the rest of the shawl across the mother's back and pass it round to her right hand, which would tuck in the remainder under the child and round her waist, thus leaving the right arm free. Men are sometimes seen nursing children in this way. It is an ancient custom and is commented upon by many travellers.

Fig. 22. Sleeves of Welsh costume. (Top) Carmarthen area. (Centre) Mid-Wales and Cardigan. (Bottom) N. Wales.

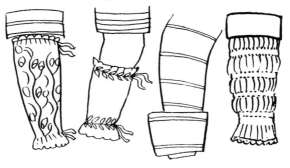

Welsh girl in the costume of part of Gwent. (N.L.W.).

Welsh girl in the costume of Cardiganshire. (N.L.W.).

Many accounts in Parish Vestry Books also give details of shawls bought to nurse children: "2s. 6d. to be given to Eliz. Williams to buy a mantle to nurse the parish child with her, and that the same be given to Margaret Williams for the same purpose; these mantles to be given up to the parish should the children die or be removed."[13]

HATS

Hats again varied a great deal. The tall, so-called "Welsh hat" was by no means universally worn; it was a fashion most prevalent in the larger towns such as Cardiff, Bangor and Carmarthen. Paintings and drawings show women wearing the tall beaver hat; while other hats are seen, too. In Gower and Penclawdd the straw was popular—of self-colour or of black. These straw hats were made locally by old women. The popularity of the flat-topped straw in Gower is accounted for by the fact that the girls carried the pails and cockle-baskets on their heads; this would have been impossible with the tall beaver hats. The straw was also more serviceable in strong coastal winds; sometimes we see it made more firm again by means of a piece of flannel or a scarf wrapped round the hat and fastened under the chin of the wearer. In North Wales a wire-brimmed straw was worn of a yellowish colour, or dyed black. It varied in shape from the Gower straw, which had more of a poke-bonnet shape.

Beaver hats also varied in shape with the locality. Those of mid-Wales were squarer in shape; while the hats of Cardigan and Pembroke were also shallower. A drawing is given of one bought at Carmarthen a hundred years ago. The price was 25/- which was prohibitive to all but the fairly well-to-do.[14] The ribbon on the hat was usually black, a band of silk or crepe and varied in width; some Carmarthen hats have a ribbon four or five inches deep; the average is about two inches, while the hats of North Wales usually had fairly narrow ribbons—an inch or

---

13. Talley Parish Vestry Book, 1835. Also Llanllwni, 1831.
14. HANES PLWYF LLANDYBIE—Rev. Gomer Roberts, M.A.

Fig. 23. (Left) Gower girls, from an old print, wearing ankle-length stockings. Note the linen pad on top of the hat. (Right) Swansea women, from Swansea decorations upon china. (G.V.).

so. The ribbon was pleated into a bow on the wearer's left. Sometimes—as in the Bangor girls'—this was extended out towards the brim, and allowed to hang down over the edge by an inch or two, the end being fringed. The inside of the hats was lined with white or grey satin, sometimes quilted. A black satin velvet or silk-crepe string was attached to each side of the hat for fastening; these strings were then tied under the chin—over the bonnet. Examples of lace made at Mydrim in 1860 are shown. (Fig. 26).

This bonnet or mob-cap was invariably worn with the hat; a muffler or kerchief would be added occasionally by Aberystwyth and Cardigan girls. These squares look like pieces of flannel pinned to the bonnet or wrapped round the head under the hat as an added protection to the neck and face in inclement weather.

Fig. 24. (Left) A hat worn at Carmarthen in the 1830's. It is a Paris make, lined with quilted red silk. A deep crepe ribbon was a sign of mourning. The bonnet has very long, double frills (C.M.) (Right) Girls of Gwent, after Lady Llanover, wearing black straws. Illustration 11 and 12. Two girls of Gwent, wearing black straws. (N.L.W.).

Bonnets were of the baby-bonnet style with two strings to tie under the chin. The extremes of style can be seen in Carmarthen and Cardigan bonnets. The Carmarthen bonnet is drawn from an authentic example in the museum and shows a made from a double piece of material—white cambric or fine calico—about six inches deep, gathered into a series of deep goffers and allowed to hang down each side of the face.[15] These frills are sewn onto a crown of the same material. The strings

15. An old verse sung round Carmarthen about 1870 refers to the large frills on caps:

> "Mae gen aunty Liza gap â las fawr,
> Las yn troi fynu a las yn troi lawr,
> A dwylath a hanner o gambric a lawn,
> Pwy dalith am rheini heb wybod i Siôn?"

Translated:

> "Aunty Liza has a cap with a large lace,
> Lace turning up and lace turning down,
> With two yards and a half of cambric and lawn,
> Who will pay for those without Siôn knowing?"

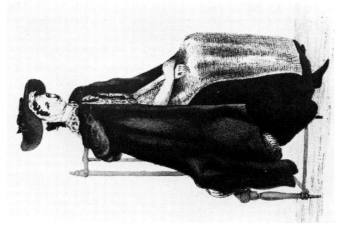

Two girls of Gwent wearing black straws (N.L.W.)

are separate, ending in oar-shaped pieces with lace edges. The Cardigan girl has a bonnet with a narrower frill, but this is continued down each string in ever-diminishing goffers. Other styles have a very short frill and the goffers are smaller. In North Wales they just show, while some have merely a lace edge to the bonnet. The bonnet is sometimes imitated in fancy dress by sewing this lace to the inside edge of the hat.

The beaver hats varied a good deal in form; those of Carmarthen, Cardiff and Swansea areas—judging by examples which have survived and by photographs and paintings of women of these times—were cone-shaped, the brim about 14 inches at its widest point and the crown about 7½ or 8 inches high, the top being about 5 inches in diameter. The section of the hat was oval. These hats were decorated with crepe ribbon or black silk braid which varied in width. Carmarthen girls liked a wide ribbon—sometimes 4 or 5 inches in depth, and this was also used to tie the hat under the chin. In parts of Cardigan and Radnor the hats were shallower and squarer in shape, tapering hardly any; while illustrations of Aberystwyth women show them wearing hats which appear to be made of fairly soft felt, which does not retain its shape very well. The Pembroke girl's hat resembles a man's beaver, which it may very well be, as many writers of the time say they are indistinguishable. The girls of Gower liked straw with flat crowns and projecting "gipsy-bonnet" front edges; these survived in modified form among cockle-gatherers until well into the present century. These hats are dealt with more fully under the descriptions of these women.

As most of these hats were made locally—of felt, beaver or straw—they can be taken, I think, as examples of peculiarly Welsh fashion. Despite the censure of the ballad-writer, who criticised the tall hats as being ugly "crocks" and "lodging for mice," they were worn in Wales during the most part of the 19th century, though they were not as universal as some romantic artists and writers would have us believe.

North Wales Women (N.L.W.)

Fig. 25. A bonnet of the mid-19th century from Glansevern, Mont. It is of pale blue, quilted satin with an outer frill of black satin. (W.F.M.)

Fig. 26. White lace made at Mydrim in 1860. (C.M.).

71

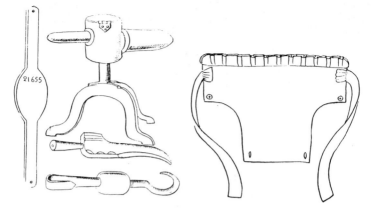

Fig. 27. (Left) A backboard, used in Laugharne in 1860. The two long pieces were fastened under the arms, the centre piece being strapped to the back. (C.M.). (Top) A goffering machine. (C.M.). (Bottom) Knitting sticks or *bachau gwregys* — "girdle hooks" — used to hold knitting wool. (W.F.M.).

Fig. 28. Pattern of a simple bonnet, worn at Abergorlech at the end of last century. The bonnet was made up by fastening the two outer corners with a button and was made of lawn, with silk ribbons.

THE APRON

The apron was universally worn and differed little from its modern counterpart. It often formed part of a servant's wages, as some of the following entries prove:

1807—Oct. 21st, Phoebe Harrie, £2. 5s., one pound of wool and a flannel apron.
1807—Oct. 22nd, Martha Perry (head maid servant) £3, one pound of wool and a flannel apron.
1815—Jemima Prosser, £4, a pound of wool and a flannel apron.

But by 1830 only the pound of wool is included in the wages of Dorothy Howell, while in 1845, Anne John, another servant, gets £2. 15s. per annum with no flannel apron or pound of wool.[16]

16. Servant's Book of John Evans of Trevayog Hall, St. Nicholas, Pem.

Gwent girl wearing apron (N.L.W.)

Another diary reveals interesting glimpses of country life early in the 19th century:

1826—Bryn y Maen, Cardigan. Sept. 14 Eclipse of the moon began at 6 p.m. Sept 28th. The sow littered seven pigs. She ate three of them.

1832—Nov. 12. Agreed with Elinor as head servant for £4 4s. and flannel for one shift. Nov. 13th. Agreed with Wm. Lewis as head servant for £6 6s. and ground to sow one bushel of potatoes.[17]

The flannel for making a shift is an interesting variation of the flannel apron donated by the master, and it is significant that by 1845 wool and flannel do not seem to be given as part of wages; this may have been because of changing fashions, or because the flannel was no longer made locally at the farm, or the servants may have purchased their aprons at the town or village.

Fig. 29. An embroidered apron of mid-19th century from Laugharne, purple, bronze and gold silks on ivory satin. (W.F.M.).

SHOES AND CLOGS

Covering for the legs and feet consisted of shoes or clogs and stockings. Shoes were by no means common among the poorer classes; even the quite respectably dressed farm servant or cockle woman was not averse to going to work or to market in her bare feet. Shoes were expensive items, much valued and cared for. The Welsh girl going to chapel or dressed for some special occasion would sometimes carry her shoes in a little box and put them on when she reached the main road, placing her

17. Diary of Thomas Jenkins. Llandeilo Fawr, 1826-32.

clogs in the box and hiding it in the hedge. The process would be repeated on her return, and she would carefully wash her feet in a wayside brook before putting on the shoes.[18]

Another writer expresses astonishment at the Welsh girls' care of their shoes. "The Welch girls of the lower order commonly go without shoes or stockings, but one would not expect to see a wench walking along a flinty road with her shoes in her hand. We could not but admire such economy."[19] Another writer records that country people used to wash their feet in a spring before going into church.[20]

Fig. 30. Farm-girls of N. Wales going to market. (Left) Wearing yellow blouse, brown skirt and white check apron, straw hat with pad, soleless stockings. (Right) Dress of dark brown and grey, straw hat, wooden-soled boots.

18. RADNORSHIRE—W. H. Howse.
19. James White: "I have heard in common with some other old parish churches—Pembrey for one—that there was a spring of clean water at the entrance to our churchyard primarily used by ones who came to church with bare feet. They were obliged to wash them before entering the church. My mother informed me she had seen it every Sunday when she was a child."
20. George Evans. TRANSACTIONS OF CARM. ANT. Vol. XV.

Because the girls had bare feet does not mean to say that their legs were bare; early drawings show the girls with sole-less stockings. Gower women are seen wearing them, and girls of North Wales too, though these stockings were longer than those of the south, having an instep which extends as far as the joint of the toes, the second toe acting as an anchor by having a loop of wool—as in the 18th century—passed round it, which served to keep the stocking in place. The colour of the stocking was black in North Wales, and grey, white or dark blue in the South, though it is not possible to make a general rule about this.

Foot-covering of the lower orders was usually the clog or wooden-soled boot. The sole was made of alder wood and men would practise the craft of clog-making as a livelihood. This is still carried on in parts of Wales, the clogs being made by the craftsman and sold mostly to farm-workers who find them by far the most satisfactory footwear for work on the land and around the farm-yard. Men and women alike wore them.

Pattens were also worn, consisting of a sole of alder wood with leather straps or uppers fastening over the instep with a buckle or lace. The ones made in the middle of the century usually had a hinge in the centre and must have been more comfortable to wear than those all on one piece. These pattens were worn by young girls and the mistress about the house as well as by farm servants. They were still in use within living memory, and I have spoken to elderly people who remember seeing them being worn when they were young.

CLOAKS

On top of her costume the Welsh girl would wear a cloak or large shawl. The whittle was more popular in Gower—and in parts of Carmarthenshire—than the cloak. In south and mid Wales the cloak was red in colour, while black and dark blue

---

26. Parish of Mount Vestry Book, 1827-28, contain among other details of money spent on Jane David: "soling her wooden shoes, 9d."

Fig. 31. Women of Caernarvon, wearing dark blue cloaks, crimson dresses, scarlet petticoats. The jacket is grey with dark blue stripes. (N.L.W.).

Fig. 32. A funeral cloak of black material, hired out at 8/- by Thomas Phillips, drapers, Lammas Street, Carmarthen. It was last used in 1890. When these cloaks were worn, funerals were considered "respecatble" (C.M.).

seem to be the most popular colours in North Wales and Cardigan. The red cloak does occur, however, in North Wales. One young man made love to to two ladies 'in red cloaks" at Bala fair. One drawing of a Bangor lady shows a child peeping out from the top part of the cloak; it seems that the child is being carried on the shoulders. When the beaver hat was worn, as walking out dress, it was possible to bring the hood of the cloak over the hat, as drawings show.

CHAPTER FOUR

COSTUMES OF LOCALITIES

To describe particular costumes of localities is now possible after the foregoing general descriptions. The girls of South Wales had much gayer costumes than their cousins of the north. The outlook and character of the South Walian may have something to do with this.

Brecon girls wore a brown or blue jacket with check stripes of a darker self-colour, check handkerchief and apron, high hat and flannel petticoat of crimson, with pin stripe of cream or black. A fuller description occurs in *Twm Shon Catti,* [1] a Welsh romantic tale of the early nineteenth century. I make no apology for quoting at length its descriptions of costume, which are generally recognised as authentic. Most of them tally with other sources I have checked, and especially with the sketches of Lady Llanover and other prints I have studied.

"There you would see the young woman of Breconshire with her pretty blushing face half hidden in a handkerchief which envelopes her head, that at first you would fancy the figure before you to be a grandmother at least. Her long linsey gown is pinned up behind, each extreme corner being joined together in the centre and confined a few inches below her waist; she has

---

1. ADVENTURES OF TWM SHON CATTI by T. Llewelyn Pritchard. Various editions.

her wooden-soled shoes for everyday and leathern ones for Sunday or for a dance, which with her stockings she takes off should a shower of rain overtake her on her journey; and when it ceases, washes her feet in the first brook she meets and puts them on again. This fair one takes especial care that her drapery should be short enough to discover her pretty ankle, and her apron sufficiently scanty to disclose her gay red petticoat with black or white stripes beneath and at the sides."

Fig. 33. Going to Market in 1861. (From the *Book of South Wales*). Fig. 33a. Brecon girl of 1870 wearing the "Joseph," a woollen wrap with fringed ends, striped in red, yellow, green, blue and black. It was worn for church-going and social occasions. (B.M.)

Glamorgan. "There you would see her extreme contrast; the Glamorgan lass in stockings cut off at the ankle and without shoes; and, although a handsome brunette with fine black eyes, dressed in a slammakin check wrapper of cotton and wool, utterly shapeless, and tied about the middle like a wheatsheaf or a faggot of wood; possessing, however, the peculiar conveniences that it could be put on in an instant, without the loss of time in dressing tastefully, and that it would fit everybody alike, as it is neither a gown nor a bed-gown, but between both and without a waist." This garment seems a direct descendant of the old Celtic *Laena* or plaid, which survived in Scotland as a garment worn by peasant women until the end of the 18th century. The description tallies with representations of this and should be considered an authentic survival of ancient dress. This was an oblong piece of cloth—the piece as made on the loom—wrapped round the figure. The mantle or whittle is the more recent example of its use, though considerably smaller.

Lady Llanover's sketches show the Glamorgan girl dressed in a neat blouse and skirt, or *betgwn* and *pais*. The *betgwn* has been curtailed to be little more than a jacket; the materials are patterned with checks and squares on a white ground—crimson is most prevalent; blue, red and black also occur, as well as plain colours. The red shawl or whittle is invariably seen. This was held in place in olden times by means of a thorn from a blackthorn. This whittle varies in length; sometimes it is quite short, reaching only to the waist; at other times it is long enough to drape round the waist and shoulders or over the head like a hooded cloak (again a survival of an ancient Celtic fashion still seen in Ireland). The colour is red or dark claret, with a striped or checked pattern in black, and there is a fringe at one end. If a pail or basket is carried on the head, a small linen pad is seen fitting the crown of the head. This appears to be a roll of padded linen. If a hat is worn, it is straw with a low crown, fitting closely to the head and a wide brim in front something like a poke bonnet. In colour it is black or natural colour.

The Gower girl wears sole-less stockings, cut off at the ankles. They appear in illustrations to be black. Their origin is probably utlitarian: working on wet sand and rocks, bare feet are the most sensible, but the ankle-length stockings give extra warmth to the legs. Stout boots are seen as well.

Penclawdd cocklewoman are similarly dressed, her dress and shawl being of a red and black colour-scheme: the shawl in checks of red and black of equal sizes, the petticoat being scarlet with narrow black stripes, her *betgwn* or blouse having

Welsh girl in the costume of Gower. (N.L.W.).

Welsh girl in the costume of Pembrokeshire. (N.L.W.).

dark crimson and black stripes. These may also be dark blue. The portrait of a cockle-woman by Evan Walters, shows her wearing such a blouse and a small, close-fitting black straw on the head.

The shawls were not always of knitted woven material; a writer of 1893 describes women of Penclawdd as wearing "turnovers—small square flannel shawls pinned low under the chin, worn by Welsh cottage women."[2]

Aberdare ladies are shown in a painting by Hugh William Williams (1829) as wearing white dresses and blue dresses, and one lady with a dark brown cloak. White hats or bonnets are worn.

Girls employed in the mines were "dressed like boys in trousers, crawling on all fours, with belts round their waists and chains passing between their legs."

Pembrokeshire girls are shown in Lady Llanover's sketches as neatly dressed with a neckerchief of dark blue, edged with a paisley pattern, a tall hat rather square in the crown, a dress of brownish stuff and a pink apron with fine black lines. In *Twm Shon Catti* the Pembrokeshire girl is described as "in her dark cloth dress of one hue, either a dark brown approximating to black or a claret colour, made by the skill of a tailor and very closely resembling the modern ladies' riding habit—a perfect picture of comfort and neatness in alliance with good taste."

Aberystwyth costumes have prevailing colours of Prussian blue in two shades. A water-colour sketch in the National Museum of Wales, Cardiff, shows a market scene in Aberystwyth in 1851. The women wear the loose gown or *bet-gwn,* reaching just below the knees, tall hats with bonnets and kerchief or muffler fastened round the back of the head as well. Some wear dark blue cloaks, while a few are smoking clay pipes. The petticoats are the same colour as the upper

2. GLIMPSES OF WELSH LIFE AND CHARACTER, Marie Trevelyan, 1893.

gowns—two shades of blue, or blue with square line of black. The kerchiefs are pale salmon-pink with squared lines·of pale blue or grey. Stockings are white, worn with black shoes. A few girls are bare-footed.

Another description of a woman seen near Devil's Bridge is from the pen of George Borrow: "wearing a kind of riding habit of blue and a high, conical hat."

Cardigan costume is also illustrated by Lady Llanover, consisting of a jacket and skirt of crimson, striped with black. The jacket has elbow-length sleeves and fits closely to the waist and shoulders. Black mittens are worn and a paisley shawl about the neck. The girl in the drawing appears to be carrying another garment, fastened around her waist. This looks like an additional jacket of a striped blue material.

In *Twm Shon Catti* another description occurs. The dress is "generally blue with red stripes and bound at the bottom with red or blue worsted caddis . . . entirely of wool solidly woven and heavy, consequently more expensive than those made of linsey or minco, or of the common inter-mixture of wool and cotton and presenting an appearance of weighty warmth equally independent of a comely cut or tasty neatness." Later "barefooted maidens" are depicted as tending an ox-drawn plough, and shoes are referred to as highly-valued, wooden clogs being generally worn by the farm girls at work.

Carmarthen girls are not depicted at all by Lady Llanover, but we have detailed descriptions from other sources. A writer of 1826[3] tells us that the "women uniformly dress alike, viz., men's hats over their white caps, blue or black and red gowns with short sleeves with linen arm covers, dark blue stockings and cloth habits or cloaks of a dark colour." On a market day he sees "Welsh women coming into the town on horseback, dressed in men's black hats, habits, coats and cloaks, with

3. Diary of M. Masleni, 1826.

saddle bags well loaded." He also met a girl of 15 or 16 years of age riding astride a pony, "with all the unconcern imaginable, with her petticoats up to her knees, her stout legs dressed in dark blue stockings." He describes the arms of some of the women "as big round as a man's leg."

Twm Shon Catti gives this picture: "Then comes the stout Carmarthen lass with thick bedgown and petticoat of a flaring brick-dust red, knitting stockings as she walks and singing a loud song as she cards or spins."

Shrewsbury district girls of the working class wore smock-frocks of "drabit"—a kind of strong twill, which would stand any weather and last a lifetime. The garments were manufactured at Llanfair. The women-folk wore garments of local manufacture—felt hats, in later times bonnets, wincey petticoats, big shawls over their shoulders and thick, woollen hose stockings with strong leather boots. Old women often wore handkerchiefs over their heads. In the upland valleys women went barefooted."[4]

North Wales girls wore more sober colourings than the South, but those who could afford to do so indulged in silks and chintzes. George Borrow describes a landlady at Cerrigy-drudion as "dressed in silks and satins with a linen coif on her head" and also a girl "in a chintz gown." These were the English fashions of the times.

Near Sycharth (Bala), he meets women "dressed in the ancient female costume, namely, a kind of round, half-Spanish hat, long blue woollen kirtle or gown, a crimson petticoat and white apron and broad, stout shoes with buckles."

The blue skirt (probably the *betgwn*) is seen also in paintings by Ibbetson, of Llangollen and Dinas Bran (1817): a girl wears a white-frilled bonnet, white blouse, white neck-cloth and blue skirt with a red petticoat showing underneath and white stockings and black shoes. A painting by Turner of Ewenny Priory,

---

4. Montgomeryshire Collections, Vol. XLVIII, part II, 1944.

Fig. 34. A Welsh wedding of 1866. Girls carry a shawl on the left arm, no flowers. The boy and girl attendants were called "shigouts."

shows a similar costume, except that the skirt is buff-coloured and the petticoat is striped vertically in white and blue.

Prints in the National Library show a variety of costumes of North Wales of about 1850. The prevailing colours are greens and blues with dark brown and an occasional dark red. Black occurs fairly frequently in stripes on aprons, pin-stripes on petticoats, etc. Bonnets are always white or cream, and the shirt or chemise is the basic garment of the same material, showing occasionally at the neck-line.

The *Bangor* girl wears cream-coloured flannel, striped with violet, Prussian blue and green. The bonnet has a deep goffering and the hat has a ribbon overhanging the front edge. Her shawl is striped with violet, and she carries a neat little melon-shaped basket with a double-handle and fitted with a lid.

The *Llanberis* girl wears not the *betgwn* but a jacket of dark brown material that appears to be very coarse and thick, with a roll collar something like a man's coat. Her hat is of brown felt, and the small bonnet underneath has a very narrow frill; she probably had little to spend on needless personal adornments.

The farm-wife wears a distinctive quilted petticoat of lavender satin under her *betgwn* and has a gay shawl chequered with green, scarlet and black. Her straw hat is wide brimmed, light yellow, and is admirably suited for country wear in the warm weather.

The winter wear of the farm-wife is shown in another drawing. Over the usual costume is worn a thick cloak with a hood, dark blue or indigo in colour. This hood was large enough to fit over the beaver hat, as many illustrations show. Pattens are worn under the shoes, raising the feet off the muddy ground.

The servant girls wear bonnets or straw hats; one shows a detachable arm-covering of linen or patterned cotton. Many pictures show servant girls wearing pattens and carrying pails, pitchers and baskets on their heads, while they walk along the roads, bare-footed, their tall hats slung by the strings to the waist.

Women of *Tan-y-bwlch* wear flannel skirts and blouses or jackets of striped material, and aprons of checks or squares. They all wear small shawls or turnovers, fastened in front or left to hang down over the shoulders, with striped or plaid patterns or paisley in tones of red, rust, orange and green. The bonnets worn under the tall hats have frilled edges about 2″ deep, the frills ending about level with the wearer's mouth. The blouses all have long sleeves, the ends being left open or gathered to meet a narrow cuff.

Women of *Radnor* are shown wearing bright scarlet cloaks with hoods. The hats are not quite as tall as those of other North Wales women, being about 7 inches in height. The white bonnets are similar. Skirts and blouses of striped flannel—dark brown or claret, with stripes and checks of black, buff and cream. Olive-green and coffee-coloured stripes are also seen. The strings tying the hats are dark brown or black, about 2″ wide, tied under the chin. Boots are worn on the feet.

The fashions persisted until the end of the century, as witnessed by Marie Trevelyan in her book, published in 1893.[5] It was in West Wales that the Welsh costumes were to be seen at their best. "There the tall beaver hat is still worn by some of the prettiest and most handsome women of the Principality. Very spick and span these women look with their short flannel skirts either of dark red or grey, plain or bob-tailed gown of grey and black or red and black Welsh flannel, V-shaped bodices, hooked—never buttoned—in front, displaying snowy lawn kerchiefs and neat turnovers, the corners of which are securely fastened at the waist by the band of the flannel apron. On their heads are pretty caps tied with fancy ribbons, and, to crown all, the tall and glossy beaver hat, which resembles an extinguisher with the fine, pointed top cut off."

This description of the hat worn in West Wales is an interesting indication of the difference between this one and those of other parts of Wales. It is apparently more pointed; examples may still be seen at the Carmarthen Museum, and in the hands of private owners in all parts of Carmarthen and Cardigan. There were, however, other hats, too, which were similar, if not actually the same as those worn in the 18th century. "Some of the women wear low flat Welsh hats of felt with straight and broad brims. There are other hats of glossy beaver, somewhat resembling those worn by the members of the Hampshire hunt." Another fashion, which we have noted earlier, also occurs: "It is by no means unusual for the elderly women to wear a kerchief over the cap and under the hat. In the winter or during wet weather, the women wear long circular cloaks, fully gathered into a hood at the neck and there fastened with a

5. GLIMPSES OF WELSH LIFE AND CHARACTER, Marie Trevelyan, 1893.

Gwent girl wearing bonnet (N.L.W.)

clasp. Some of these cloaks have moveable hoods, long enough to be drawn over the same high beaver hats."

Our authoress then goes on to particularize the dress of the different women. "Cottage women always wear aprons of Welsh flannel, which are large and comfortable. They are to be had in grey and black, black and white and a mingling of all. Over their shoulders in the winter-time, they wear small square flannel shawls called "turnovers," folded cornerwise and pinned rather low under the chin. On their heads they wear neat sun-bonnets of printed calico, under which the old women wear prim caps tied with black or coloured fancy ribbons. Welsh flannel dresses are still much worn, though they are being rapidly superseded by woollen and cotton fabrics of English manufacture."[6] This paragraph gives us a few more details about the large variety of headgear worn; the fact that it is only the older women who wear the bonnets should be noted; these bonnets gradually disappeared altogether, being first discarded, it appears, by the younger women.

Cocklewomen are then described; they wear "short gowns of red and black flannel, which are turned up in front and pinned close under the waist at the back . . . (they) display neat short petticoats of Welsh flannel aprons in front. On their heads they wear small Welsh hats, suitable for bearing the weight of the cockle pails. A thick pad, known as a *dorch,* protects both the hat and the head from the pail. These untrimmed hats are of black straw with a fancy edge. They come slightly forward over the forehead and recede to the back of the head where they are turned up and curved. The only head-covering somewhat resembling it was the one known as the 'gipsy-hat' and bonnet in the old fashion-plates of 1872." This description of the cocklewoman's head-covering is very interesting; and is perhaps a relic of very ancient times. The circular pad, the *dorch* may have been of Flemish origin; there is a French word *torche* which means a pad on the head for carrying

6. GLIMPSES OF WELSH LIFE AND CHARACTER, Marie Trevelyan, 1893.

loads. The similarity is too close to be merely accidental, though I have not seen any explanation of the word *dorch*. Of course, this may be the mutated form (Welsh would say *y dorch*—and not *y torch*), the word being pronounced in the Welsh way. On the other hand, it may be derived from the word torque which is similar in shape.

Marie Trevelyan gives another brief note about the dress of the cocklewomen: "The dresses are made with short and shaped fronts, disclosing snowy neckerchiefs, and some of the elderly women wear neat white caps under the small Welsh hats."

The dress of the *Pembroke* woman is described as "very dark brown or deep claret-coloured habit cloth, which fit like a glove and their low shoes are of fine leather." This is quite close to the earlier descriptions and drawings. The only difference is the allusion to the shoes.

Cardigan women, who "for the most part are thick-set and short of stature, wear dark blue flannel gowns with red stripes. These are bound round the bottom with solidly-woven red or blue wool caddis, making the gowns, which are somewhat destitute of fit and neatness, heavy and comfortable. These women are always clogged and generally cloaked." The drawing of Lady Llanover is fairly close to this description.

Carmarthen girls are dressed in "thick dresses resembling bedgowns and petticoats of red brick-coloured flannel, sometimes with a pin-mark stripe of black or white." This pattern may still be seen in the country districts in the flannel woven in the rural mills.

"*Brecon* women generally envelop their heads in a kerchief and their long, linsey gowns or kirtles are turned up in front and pinned at the back just a few inches below the waist. They have wooden clogs for everyday wear and leathern shoes for Sunday, and, as they boast of neat ankles, it is the rule among them to let them be visible beneath short petticoats of bright red or crimson flannel with black or white stripes. They also

An early print of various Welsh Costumes (N.L.W.)

wear smaller flannel aprons than the women of the other shires." This description tallies very closely with that of Richard in earlier times.

The shapeless dress of the *Glamorgan* girl, referred to by the above writer, is again commented upon by Miss Trevelyan. "In days gone by the Glamorgan women, who were considered very handsome, did not care so much for dress. They favoured gowns made of material in which cotton and wool were intermixed. These gowns were made like loose wrappers and with

Welsh Costume showing the enormity of some tall hats (N.L.W.)

93

out waists. Flannel aprons were worn with these, and the woman's feet were enclosed in thick lamb's wool stockings and wooden clogs. Leather shoes were worn only on Sundays and holidays. Glamorgan and Breconshire women were not so particular about dress as those of other shires, because they frequently had to work on the farms and out in the fields just like the men."

CHAPTER FIVE

MEN'S COSTUMES

The costume of Welshmen of the 19th century does not differ a great deal from that of general fashions in England; only in the rural areas do we find evidence of the use of homespun cloths and some fashions of a bygone age still surviving. In 1873, a man giving evidence before the Royal Commission on Land in Wales was asked: "You do not find men wearing suits of clothes made from wool from their own farms?" and replied: "Oh, yes, sometimes, but that is not the rule. They are considered the best clothing and the strongest whatever for wear." This shows the trend of fashions at the end of the century.

In the earlier years, homespun cloth was frequently worn, probably more from necessity than choice among country people. George Borrow meets a man near Bala "dressed in white coat, corduroy breeches, shoes and grey worsted stockings" and also sees a farmer's son "in white great coat."[1] This white material was the familiar homespun, undyed cloth—frieze.

The corduroy trousers were universally worn. In the same book is described a labourer near Bangor wearing "blue coat and corduroy trousers" and a man at Pentraeth Coch "in a brown jerkin and corduroy trousers with a broad, low-crowned buff-coloured hat on his head, and what might be called half shoes and half high-lows on his feet. He had a short

1. WILD WALES. George Borrow.

Fig. 35. (Left) Welsh miners of last century, from "The Book of South Wales" (Centre) A Carmarthen sportsman. (C.M.). He wears a coat of dark blue cloth, with gilt buttons and buckled belt, brown breeches, black hat and shoes. (Right) A Welsh farmer, wearing homespun coat and breeches, grey stockings yellow waistcoat, black shoes and hat. (N.L.W.).

pipe in his mouth."[2] A drover is dressed in "pepper and salt coat of the Newmarket cut, breeches of corduroy and brown top-boots, and on his head a broad, black coarse, low-crowned hat. In his left hand he held a heavy whale-bone whip with a brass head." These drovers of North Wales often used a Liverpool expression—"to box Harry"—which meant to have high tea, bacon and eggs, etc., instead of dinner.

2. Ibid.

A description of farmers and farm-hands is contained in *Twm Shon Catti*. In one of his numerous disguises the hero "now appeared in a sober grey suit, shining black shoes with buckles, stockings of the wool of a black sheep and a knitted Welsh wig[3] of the same that fitted like a skull-cap and concealed every lock of his hair. Thus arrayed, he presented the appearance of a grave puritanical mountain farmer from the remote district of Cardiganshire."

A farm-hand is described as follows: "His feet were thrust into a very heavy pair of clogs or wooden-soled shoes, which, being stiff and large, maintained such a haughty independence of their inmates as to need being tied on with a hay-band. His legs were enveloped in a pair of wheat-stalk leggings or bands of twisted straw, winding round and round and covering them from knee to ankle. A raw hairy cow-hide formed the material of his inexpressibles, which were loose, like a trousers cut at the knee; and his jerkin was of a brick-dust red with black stripes like the faded garb of the Carmarthenshire woman. A load of red locks, quite innocent of the slightest acquaintance with a comb, the whole surmounted with a soldier's cast-off Monmouth cap, so highly varnished with grease as to appear waterproof. Without any apology for a waistcoat he wore a blue flannel shirt, striped with white, open from the chin to the waistband, which answered the purpose of a cupboard, to contain his enormous cargo of bread and cheese and leeks." The details of the straw gaiters are probably authentic, as is most of the rest of the costume for that of a farm labourer, although one can discount a little of the exaggeration of the consciously comic portrait. Straw was also used as garters. A later note to a song describes a girl buying red garters at Cardigan fair to replace the straw ones her lover is wearing. These garters were made on fireside machines and were of plain colour or woven

---

3. A close-fitting knitted cap, worn in cold weather.

in checks of two colours, blue and white or black and white being generally seen.

Fig. 36. (Left) A cream satin waistcoat with dark brown embroidery. (W.F.M.). (Above) A gartermaking machine, using two colours manipulated on the hearth. (C.M.).

In the district between Shrewsbury and Aberystwyth the farmers wore a "coarse, striped kind of woollen" cloth, tall, beaver hats of local manufacture, white or coloured waistcoats and long-tailed coats below the knees. An old gentleman is described, "He wore an old beaver hat, a coat of blue cloth with bright gilt buttons, of the swallow-tail cut, white silk waistcoat and white knee-breeches, and white silk stockings and shoes with silver buckles. Under his arm, whatever the weather, would be a green umbrella with buck horn handle."[4]

Near Lampeter another rural character, somewhat more disreputable is described as "a singular looking figure mounted on a dirty half-starved Welch pony with a piece of cord round its nose by way of a bridle, (who) issued from the wood close by me. The man was about 5 feet 2 inches high, looked about seventy, his beard full six months growth, his skin the colour of excrement, an old, patched, drab-coloured coat, no shirt, a ragged handkerchief round his neck, a pair of greasy leather

4. HISTORY OF LLANFAIR PARISH, E. Pentyrch Gittins.

breeches patched with sheep's skin with the wool on, and large pack-boots, with a cole-heaver's hat on."[5]

The leather breeches were considered elegant wear for a rural buck, who is described in *Twm Sion Cati* as being so attired, and also wearing a red neck-cloth.

Other cloths were the blue of local manufacture—"blue frieze"[6] grey or drab-coloured cloth of the Brecon area, and grey woollen cloth of Radnor and Prestatyn, which was highly valued for its durability and warmth. The "Grey Coat Club" was formed in 1851 to perpetuate the wearing of this grey cloth in the Rhyl and Prestatyn areas; meetings were held at these towns, the members wearing grey coats and waistcoats with crested buttons. The club had Whig tendencies and was active for about ten years.

The woollen stockings were hand-knitted by the wives or mothers and were durable and highly valued. So much so indeed that they received royal patronage; George III had a pair of woollen stockings knitted for him by a vicar's daughter of Trawsfynydd, near Bala. The King wore these and found them very comfortable. Another knitted commodity already mentioned is the "Welsh wig." This was a skull-cap, popular with coach passengers because of its warmth. It was worn under the hat and large numbers were made for sale in the Bala district. Black wool (from the black sheep) seems to have been the most popular wear, though blue and grey are also mentioned.

The shirts were of flannel or of homespun linen. Flax was grown locally for these.[7] The flax shirt was regarded as the proper wear for working men, and wearers of other shirts were despised. "When a farmer appeared at a 'reap' in a cotton shirt, he was looked upon as a foreigner and was ashamed to take off his coat like the other men who appeared in their

5. Diary of Capt. Jenkin Jones, May 17th, 1819.
6. WILD WALES, George Borrow.
7. HISTORY OF RADNOR, W. H. Howse.

flaxen shirts."[8] There follows a cautionary tale of a young man who got married in a cotton shirt, caught pneumonia and died.

Linen was used too for the making of smocks worn by shepherds. These men of Cardigan wore long-sleeved smocks with smocking on the chest and cuffs. A farmer who fought at Waterloo wore at work a smock with two pockets with buttons, cuffs fastening with two bone buttons and with a neck opening fastening with four buttons. Paintings of these times show the smocks as reaching to just below the knees of the wearer. Smocks were worn at milking times as well as by shepherds. It was considered best to wash them with rain water to preserve the quality of the material.

The farm-hand kept his clothing in a wooden box or chest under his bed, and the box was carefully locked and kept clean, the repository of all his precious belongings. He would take this box with him if he changed his place at the beginning of May or end of September, the normal times for hiring farm-servants.

Towards the end of the century clothing of farm-workers varied a little. Those of North Wales are described[9] as wearing whipcord breeches and a black jacket with a white overall on top. Felt leggings of fawn coloured leather were worn, with brown pearly buttons up one side. Gamekeepers wore waistcoats made of real mole-skin. These have turned-back collars and four pockets. Hedgers use thick leather gloves, made locally, and harvest workers wore "little leather cushions" strapped to the knees, padded with woollen cloth to protect them when kneeling at work. These pads were also used when ferreting. A similar practice was resorted to by Carmarthen countrymen; mole-catchers used to strap to their knees the leather pad, illustrated.[9a] It consisted of a cylinder of stiff leather—rather like a top-hat in shape—with a piece sewn onto

8. HISTORY OF THE PARISH OF LLANBADARN FAWR, Rev. A. Jordan.
9. WANDERINGS IN NORTH WALES, Cledwyn Hughes.
9a. See below p 101.

Fig. 37. Purses from Carmarthen, used in the 19th century. (Top) Olive plush, embroidered with pink and green. (Centre) Crocheted green silk. (Bottom) Crocheted dark brown silk with silver beads. (W.F.M.). (Lower) A mole-catcher's knee-pad of leather, strapped to the knee as a protection. (C.M.).

the end to fit the knee; straps were sewn on each side to fasten round the leg.

A postman carried (at Anglesey—though probably typical of the rest of Wales, too)[10] "leathern wallet, walking stick and bugle" and was accompanied by a "terrier dog". He wore a "black, glazed hat."[11]

Policemen seen at Llangollen fair wore "blue coats and leather hats, holding their thin walking stick behind them."[12]

A Snowdon ranger and guide wore a "smock and a hairy cap"[13] made from the fur of the goat. The landlord of a tavern near the Devil's Bridge also wore a fur cap.

---

10. Charles Dickens, 1858.
11. WILD WALES, George Borrow.
12. Ibid.
13. Ibid.

An itinerant preacher is described[14] as "a brisk man, wearing a grey coat of homespun cloth, a many-coloured jacket, corduroy knee-breeches, stockings of black wool and wooden boots. He rode a red cob." The boots were probably clogs.

Fishermen and sailors near Tenby at the beginning of the century wore short blue or red coats and white breeches. Some were bare-legged, others are seen with white stockings and black shoes.[15] Later, long white trousers were worn, with short jackets.

Fig. 38. Tenby fishermen of about 1820, from a painting by Charles Norris. They wear blue coats or jackets, grey trousers, dark brown or black hats. Blue trousers are also seen and wooden-soled clogs. (T.M.)

Night attire consisted usually of a flannel shirt—quite often that worn during the day by the poorer classes. The custom of going to bed in day-clothing—or in the basic garments persisted among poorer people up to modern times; while there are also examples mentioned by Captain Jenkin Jones.[16] His bedroom companion was an elderly man, who, after supper, "undressed entirely" on going to bed. The bed itself consisted of straw laid on a few boards, covered with a blanket. This was at an inn near Beddgelert.

---

14. Biography of Siencyn Penhydd.
15. TENBY CASTLE, a painting by Nicholas Pocock, 1821.
16. Diary of Captain Jenkin Jones, 1819.

The price of men's shirts, etc., may be gathered from the following list. It is printed and was presumably issued to prospective buyers:[17]

"Thread to be charged for if not sent"

	s	d
Making a fine Shirt, trimmed	1	6
Untrimmed do. from 10d. to	1	0
Striped Calico and Dowlais Shirts[18]		6
Boys fine shirts, trimmed	1	0
Do., untrimmed from 6d. to		8
Fine Shirts, trimmed		9
Wrist bands per pair		2
Pockets, per pair		2
Collar		2

Shirts were also made by the children of St. Peter's School, Carmarthen. They are included in a list of articles sent as a "contribution towards the relief of the sick and wounded in the Franco-Prussian war" in 1870.

Some eccentrics, of course, wore their shirts differently from the rest of the men. Dr. Price, of Pontypridd, appeared at the Court of Common Appeal in 1873 with his shirt worn outside his vest, without any necktie. The rest of his costume consisted of green trousers and a long, green cloak lined with scarlet, clasped at the throat and vandyked at the edges. His portrait shows him with long hair and beard, white, tipped with yellow, and a cap which appears to consist of fur skins sewn together.

Laundry was included in the payments made for the keeping of paupers. A Parish Account of 1833 reads, "agreed to pay the sum of five pounds to James James for keeping, clothing and washing of William Roberts to the 25th of March next to commence 25th December previously, and also to keep him confined from trespassing upon anyone by HANDCUFFING OR CHAINING." The latter stipulation seems rather harsh treatment even to a felon, which is an indication of the inhumane methods of a hundred years ago.

---

17. GOLDEN GROVE, 1834. List Printed by T. & H. Williams, Printers, Llandilo.
18. Dowlais or Dowlass—a kind of coarse calico, named after the town in Brittany (Daoulas) where it was manufactured.

Shirts worn by miners were almost invariably of dark blue flannel, still seen today. This flannel was also made up into drawers, which are slightly different in cut from regulation men's underwear. These flannel pants are still worn by countrymen, usually the more elderly. The rest of the collier's dress consisted of leather jerkin, leather cap with a peak, and long corduroy trousers. There was a candle socket in front of the cap. Illustrations of the collier of a hundred years ago show him carrying strapped to his back a kind of basket, into which he filled the coal. Later in the century the corduroy trousers gave way to that of moleskin. The trouser is tied round just under the knee. I once asked an old collier what this was for, and he replied: "To keep the dust out of my eyes." The reason is that, when kneeling at the coal-face, dirt and small coal are apt to get inside the trouser-leg and work their way up with uncomfortable results. This tying of the trouser just below the knee prevents this. A piece of string, or a leather strap or thong was also adopted. The strap or thong was called a "york".

The underground haulier also had his peculiar costume. With basic garments as above, he also wore a piece of leather across his backside, suspended from or fastened to his leather belt. This square or oblong piece of leather was called *pishin tin lledr* — "leather piece for the backside"—and was a protection when hoisting trams, using his back to help in the lifting. This was part of his work, coupling or uncoupling trams when supplying coal-workers with empties. Very often a small strap was worn round the neck, too, onto which a lamp could be hooked. Mufflers of all kinds were worn.

In the matter of footwear, the South varied a little from the North. Leather boots were worn in the South, whereas wooden clogs were worn in the North. Colliers of Wrexham are so described.[19]

---

19. WANDERINGS IN NORTH WALES, Cledwyn Hughes.

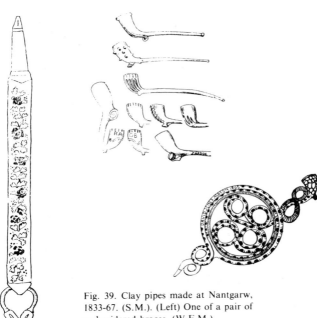

Fig. 39. Clay pipes made at Nantgarw, 1833-67. (S.M.). (Left) One of a pair of embroidered braces. (W.F.M.).

Tin workers had a dress very much the same as that of the miners, except that lighter clothing would be worn, consisting of everyday clothing that had gone shabby. They wore mufflers—very often just a narrow strip of cloth—and also a band of cloth round the forehead to prevent the perspiration from running into the eyes. Long aprons were worn, too. At work, only a trouser and thin vest would be worn—sometimes only a trouser. Clogs were the usual footwear, as leather-soled boots might be burnt by hot metal. A leather piece would be worn on the hand; this piece would be strapped round and faced with a metal palm, used for separating the sheets of tin by striking the corner of the "box" (mass of sheets) with the palm of the hand.

Men's pipes are shown, made at the Nantgarw factories in Swansea, 1833-67, and with fanciful decorations to suit the calling or tastes of the smoker; the farrier or drover would have the one with a little hoof, the footballer the one with a ball and foot, the member of the Royal and Ancient Order of Buffaloes that with the initials R.A.O.B., and the member of the Hearts of Oak that with oak leaves, etc.

Oak-leaves were a favourite motif in embroidery. The illustration shows a pair of braces, embroidered with roses and oak-leaves. Braces were not quite the same shape as modern ones, as is shown in the sketch.

Purses were of silk or cord, often embroidered.